# Able Writers in

## Developing the potential of gifted children in primary schools:

## A practical guide for teachers

'...the growth of our imagination
is central to the growth of our intelligence.'

Andrew Motion, Poet Laureate

by Brian Moses and Roger Stevens

# Brilliant
PUBLICATIONS

*For Paul Chandler, Head Teacher of St. James' CE Junior School, Tunbridge Wells, with thanks for his support and encouragement.*

Published by Brilliant Publications

Unit 10, Sparrow Hall Farm, Edlesborough, Dunstable,
Bedfordshire LU6 2ES, UK

tel:       01525 222292
e-mail:    info@brilliantpublications.co.uk
website: www.brilliantpublications.co.uk

The name Brilliant Publications and its logo are registered trade marks.

Written by Brian Moses and Roger Stevens
Cover and inside illustrations by Brett Hudson
Copyright © Brian Moses and Roger Stevens 2008
Printed ISBN: 978 1 903853 99 3
ebook ISBN:  978 0 85747 202 1

Printed in the United Kingdom

The Publisher would like to thank the following organisations for permission to use various
material mentioned in this book:

'Thirteen Ways of Looking at a Blackbird', from *The Collected Poems of Wallace Stevens* by
Wallace Stevens, copyright 1954 by Wallace Stevens and renewed 1982 by Holly Stevens.
Used by permission of Alfred A Knopf, a division of Random House, Inc.

'The Trouble with Geraniums', from *A Book of Nonsense* by Mervyn Peakes, first published by
Peter Owen in 1972 and reissued in 1999. Used by permission from the Mervyn Peake Estate.

'The Locust Tree in Flower (first version)' from *Collected Poems: 1909-1939, Volume* 1 by
William Carlos Williams. Copyright (c) 1938 by New Directions Publishing Corp., Reprinted by
permission of New Directions Publishing Corp and Carcanet Press.

The Poetry Society for allowing us to include ideas adapted from *Jumpstart* by Cliff Yates on
pages 28 and 85.

# Main Contents

# Introduction

## What an 'able writer' is and why we wrote this book

Many children have a real ability for writing. Not only are their technical skills well developed, but they also have a flair for taking risks with their writing. They are capable of stretching their imaginations, making connections and looking at things in different ways.

Able writers are children who have probably read a lot and absorbed much and who can use all this as a launch pad for their own ideas – not just regurgitating the plot of last night's horror film, but finding a new slant and taking a different perspective that is often totally original. We all know these children and at times feel in awe of them. Were we capable of doing what they do when we were their age?

These are the children who won't put their hands in the air to ask, 'Is it all right if I put this, Miss?' They will quietly and confidently take an idea where they want to take it. If there is a framework for a piece of writing, they will quickly see its limitations. Sometimes they will adapt the framework and bend it in the direction they want to go. On other occasions they will simply abandon it and yet still show that they understand the intention of the lesson. It is this ability to surprise the teacher that makes working with able writers so exciting.

This book is designed for teachers who want to develop the potential of their gifted pupils. It passes on ideas and practical advice, including lesson plans and examples of children's work, which we have found to work well with the groups of able writers that we have taught over the last few years. As writers, we often work with groups consisting of children from different schools who come together for a day. For more about the Able Writers Project, see our Endword.

*Note: the poem on page 5 is a superb example of the kind of work able writers can produce. It is essentially a first draft produced by an eleven year old.*

### The Firework Girl
*by Emily*

The firework girl is what she is,
just waiting to explode.
Everything about her is a firework.

Her brain is a green and silver one,
It whirls around a Catherine wheel,
Always full in for a chance to grow and grow until...

**BANG!**

an idea pops out of the cycle completely and utterly unique.
Her brain is a green and silver one.

Her temper is another thing, a red and gold rocket,
Soaring upwards always at a peak ready to shoot and spin up and up,
Waiting for someone or something to really set her off then...

**BOOM!**

Whoever set her off is in for a dreadful, frightful, terrifying shock!
Her temper is another thing, a red and gold rocket.

Her friendliness is a blue and purple sparkler,
Bright and fizzy with light.
Dazzling brightly waiting to meet with someone to ignite,
But a lot of people are buckets of cold water,
Evil as they douse and

**POP!**

There's nothing left to fizz,
No friendliness left.
Her friendliness is a blue and purple sparkler!

Her dramaticness is a multicoloured one completely bonkers,
Sparky, beautiful and totally believable,
With bits and pieces everywhere it's a display of madness,
and of beauty and intelligence bright and emotional,
Because as she goes on stage she is the firework,
She is the character she is performing
And then...

**BOOM BANG ZOOM!**

Her dramaticness is a multicoloured one completely bonkers!

So you see her life is a box of amazing stunning extraordinary fireworks and
Bright funky flashes,
Just waiting to explode!
So stay away, beware this box is highly dangerous,
Who knows what will

**JUMP OUT?**

# Getting Started:
# Poetry & Prose

# Redrafting

## Some essentials

Redrafting is a process that children quite often find difficult. Teachers sometimes find it hard to give them the help that is crucial to honing a piece of work from something good into something excellent.

There are a number of things that we're looking at when we try to help a child with a piece of writing. For example: Does the writing really communicate the child's ideas to the reader? Does a poem maintain a consistent rhythm? More obviously, is the spelling and punctuation correct? (Spelling and punctuation are less important in the early stages of a piece of writing when we are concentrating on creativity, helping a child to get her ideas from her head onto paper, but these more prosaic matters become important when it comes to the final draft.) How is the sound of the words and the way the piece flows? Are there words that interrupt the flow? If so these might simply need taking out.

All writers, when they've worked hard at something, are usually dismayed at the idea of losing words or even whole sentences. It is important that able writers learn that what is being taken out can be as crucial as what is left in when it comes to perfecting a piece of writing. Knowing what should stay and what should go is the essence of editing, and it's useful for children to learn that while they should be able to edit their own work, the contribution of others can be just as valuable.

We always tell children that our wives look at our poems before they go to our publishers. We explain that when you write a poem, you're often too close to it, too protective of it, and you need someone else to stand back and look at the piece in a less emotional way.

Quite often your critic will say she likes particular words, but then she'll point out a phrase that she doesn't like or she thinks doesn't quite fit. This can be a line that you really like and are desperate to keep in. When this happens to Brian he heads off for his office to sit and sulk. Roger always argues the point. But quite quickly we realise that our partners are right and it is our obstinacy that is holding back the completion of the poem.

Children find it interesting to know that writers of novels, too, have to suffer the indignity of having whole sections cut by their editors, who also often demand complete rewrites. It's not uncommon to have to rework almost a whole novel. When you're talking about rewriting several months' work you can imagine how that feels. But the best writers – the ones your pupils probably enjoy reading – will know that ultimately it is for the novel's good. An experienced editor will usually be able to see things that you can't, weaknesses of plot for example or flabby prose. Professional writers soon learn not to be precious about their work.

## Response partners

Able writers are capable of acting as 'response partners' and this can be of real value in helping children to look critically at each other's work.

When organising groups of response partners it is often best if children keep to the same partner. This can lead to the development of mutual trust. Children should understand before working together that their responses to another's work should be considered carefully and offered in a positive way which will help improve the piece of work and not just criticise it. As writers themselves they should be reminded that negative criticism is very rarely of any use.

Give children a step-by-step plan. Ask them to read each other's work through, reading silently at first and then aloud to each other. These readings will often reveal any problems with the flow or rhythm of the pieces. Suggest that the first response should always be one of encouragement, they should try to find something they like, a line or a word, and mention that before anything else.

After praising their partner they can begin the more constructive criticism: Is there a line that doesn't quite fit? Does it need to be scrapped or could it benefit from a little rejigging? Are there dull words that could be replaced with more interesting or ambitious ones? Is the same word used too many times? Does the piece sound good when it is read aloud or can anything be done to improve it?

Once this process has been followed, then the two children involved should get together with their teacher and talk about each other's work. To start with, this discussion will almost certainly be teacher-led, but as children become more experienced critics they will begin to display more initiative.

## The teacher's input

Of course, the rules are the same and you must practise what you preach: Start with encouragement for a good word, an interesting phrase, a clever idea. This will make it easier for the writer to accept that there is still work to do. Similarly, always finish with a word of encouragement – 'Once you've sorted that out then this will be a really good piece of work.' An atmosphere of encouragement and of mutual respect for each other as writers is of vital importance.

Another factor to emphasise is that the writing isn't being changed because it is wrong. It is rather a matter of sifting through words and ideas to find those which are best. Some parts that are rejected initially may well be reinstated later on – either in this piece of writing or even in another. For this reason discourage rubbing out and try to insist on crossing out. If a child is working on a computer, get her to save the first copy and work on a second.

Look for those words and phrases that could be trimmed, perhaps because they mean the same thing or because they spoil the flow of the writing. Perhaps there are better words that might be used. Ask the children to suggest what these might be. If children are shown how to use a thesaurus they may find words which convey more precisely the feeling they are trying to communicate. Sometimes words sound particularly good when used together and techniques such as alliteration can be discussed and employed to good effect.

### Clichés

Discuss whether something is a cliché. Clichés are lazy writing, they are words and phrases that have been used far too many times. As writer and broadcaster Clive James once wrote in his **Observer** column: '...the essence of a cliché is that words are not just misused, but have gone dead.'

So help the children to look for clichés, for example **the dog was barking his head off**, **cotton-wool clouds**, **white as a sheet**. Talk about what makes them clichés and how they can be replaced or at least freshened up. There are one or two exercises you could try with your writers later in this book. It's also worth remembering not to be too hard on the children here.

Although you will recognise a cliché – your writers will not have read as much as you, nor will they necessarily have come across some of these phrases before. Even if a description has been in use for many, many years, the first time you read it, it is new to you!

For more on clichés, see page 127.

## Use of adjectives

All through their school lives, and rightly so, children are encouraged by their teachers to make use of as many different adjectives as possible. This can lead to children going completely OTT! You sometimes have to hurdle a whole list of adjectives to reach a noun – the silent, spooky, sleepy, eerie, gloomy graveyard. Frequently the adjectives will work against one another, or mean the same thing, eerie/spooky, for example. Point out how one carefully selected adjective is often far more effective.

# Warming up

## Some useful techniques

We're used to seeing sports people and performers warming up. Footballers skip up and down the touchline before coming onto the pitch; athletes stretch and bend; singers test their vocal cords with a scale or two. With our 'able writers' groups, where the children are sometimes strangers and feeling a little apprehensive, we use the following warm-up exercises to create a positive, can-do atmosphere in the group. But they are also suitable to use if you are planning a long session with any group of children. They help to get the mind in gear. Additionally, these exercises can be extended and used as full-scale lessons in their own right.

• Make your confession

Tell the children that you are going to confess to something you've done in the past. For example: *When my granddad came to stay he left his false teeth in a glass of water in our bathroom. I picked them up to look at them but the glass slipped from my grasp and the teeth fell into the toilet bowl. I fished them out and gave them a quick rinse before putting them back in the glass. I meant to tell him in the morning but I overslept. By the time I got downstairs, Granddad was eating his breakfast!*

Confessions like this can easily become the starting point for stories and children can be encouraged to think of their own examples. Have any of them escaped punishment by hiding the evidence of an accident, or by blaming a sister, brother, friend, dog or cat?

**My Confession**
*by Emily*

Can you keep a secret?
Good!
Okay, here goes.
It wasn't Andrew who let the rabbit out,
even though I said it was, I lied.
I let Silka out because she looked so alone and sad
left in the class during break time.
So I liberated her, let her run wild and free.
Then the bell rang, which meant trouble for me.
We came in and she was sitting on the desk chewing up our
  homework.
The teacher said, "Who did it?"
And I blamed Andrew Slater.
But I felt guilty and really bad!
So there you go, I've told you now, so I hope you can keep a
  secret.

**My Confession**

*by Anna-Leigh*

It was 2 in the morning and I went downstairs for a glass of milk. That's when I saw them – the chocolates that my dad got my mum for her birthday. It was tempting so I took them down and ate seven of them. There were three left. In the morning we were all downstairs and my family found out that seven were missing. As we all turned round my brother got tempted and nicked a chocolate. We all saw him and he got the blame.

* Total mega embarrassment!

Similarly, embarrassing moments can be turned to good use. Ask the children if they can remember a time when they were really embarrassed. Tell them you mean not just red-faced, shuffle-your-feet, change-the-subject embarrassed but more I-can't-go-on-existing-after-what-has-happened embarrassed. It's that moment when you're swimming and you think there's seaweed caught round your ankles and you flick it free. Then you realise that what you thought was seaweed was actually your swimming trunks and now you've kicked them away you can't find them. There is a very crowded beach between you and your towel.

Or it's the time you're sitting on the bus going on about how stupid and ugly and pointless your mate is, only to turn round and find that mate's mother sitting behind you.

That is total mega embarrassment!

Children can focus on one particular embarrassing moment and describe it or perhaps list a series of such moments in a poem:

*If my whole life flashed before me*
*I wouldn't want to remember*
*The day my dad took his trousers off in public*
*because a wasp had got inside them*
*The moment I took hold of someone's hand in the supermarket*
*and it wasn't Mum's*
*The journey when we found ourselves driving along*
*an airport runway*
*The meal when I spilt gravy all over dad's important business guest*
*And worst of all*
*Being made to hold my teacher's hand because I'd misbehaved on the way*
*to swimming lesson*

## • Feeling frightened

Encouraging the children to remember a time when they were frightened can often kick-start a poem or story. Children can list things that they would like to do but are too frightened to attempt. Brian's list would include riding on a roller coaster and taking a trip on a boat for anything longer than the Isle of Wight crossing. Roger's would certainly feature finding himself at the top of the Empire State Building or climbing a mountain. Thinking about their fears and the way they react to them may help your writers understand themselves a little more and act as a stimulus for a piece of work.

**Tornado Chasing**
*by Lucy*

I'd like to feel the racing wind,
I'd like to see the lightning.
I'd like to test the tornado's patience
and cure my phobia of storms.

I'd like to do this
but guess what,
I won't!

### I'm Far Too Scared!

*by Josie*

There are many things I'd love to do –
but the problem is I'm far too scared.
I'd love to swim alongside sharks, the assassins of the sea,
but I can't, I'm far too scared.
I'd love to jump off the high board and feel the air
whip past me as I plunge to the water below,
but I can't, I'm far too scared.
I'd love to sing and dance on a stage with fancy costumes
and shakers, in front of a clapping crowd,
but I can't, I'm far too scared.
I'd love to stand up to bullies rather than receiving
a round red nose and a black eye,
but I can't, I'm far too scared.
I'd love to do what I feel when I feel
rather than bottling up all my emotions,
but I can't, I'm far too scared.
There are many things I'd love to do –
but I can't
I'm – far – too – scared.

### I Want to Ride Nemesis Inferno
*by Monique*

I want to ride Nemesis Inferno,
It's here at Thorpe Park.
I don't care about the sissy rides,
the teacups and all of that lark.

I want to ride Nemesis Inferno,
feel the wind rush through my hair.
I get up close and then I stop
and stare and stare and stare.

I want to ride Nemesis Inferno,
ride it right to the top
and then rush down that steep, steep hill
dropping, dropping, drop.

I want to ride Nemesis Inferno,
feel the lonely breeze,
but then at the start time
I absolutely freeze.

I want to ride Nemesis Inferno,
It would be really fun.
I'm just about to get on
but then I see my mum.

I want to ride Nemesis Inferno,
but now I'm going home.
I'm going to ride Nemesis Inferno,
Well, next time anyway!

• Crossing the river

Tell the class that they are standing on the bank of a river. The river is as wide as the classroom. Ask them to suggest ways to get to the other side. As they make suggestions – write them on the board.

This is a brainstorming session and you are encouraging the children to be as wild and imaginative as possible. If their idea will get them across the divide – that's fine.

You should end up with thirty or forty suggestions! These might range from – *cross over by bridge, swim, go by boat* – to these suggestions from a group of Year 7 writers in Battle, East Sussex.

• *Join a circus and borrow the clown's stilts.*
• *Blow up a puffer fish with helium and float across.*
• *Cross using a pair of ancient Greek winged sandals.*
• *Cross the river by standing on the tongue of a whale.*
• *Wait for a very cold day, then – when the river freezes – skate across.*
• *Catch a lift with the Flying Monkeys.*

That was a great group to work with!

Discuss with your group or class the order of lines in a poem like this. They might like to put the obvious things first and the most crazy suggestion last. You might also discuss rhythm and rhyme. Would your poem lend itself to either?

Brainstorm ideas for a poem such as:

• *Ten ways to get out of doing homework, (a popular suggestion)*
• *Seventeen ways to climb over a wall.*
• *Eleven ways to help Mum.*
• *Things to do when you're really bored.*

Here are some ideas which children have produced:

**Ways to Train a Pigeon**
*by Jessie*

Give it some food and then throw it up in the air.
Tie it to a piece of string and pull the string up and down.
Throw it out of a plane and hope it survives.
Talk to it calmly then throw it out of a plane with a parachute.
Get some tiny pigeon rocket boots and attach them on.
Stuff it in a bottle of pop, shake it up, and hope it lands in Australia.

**Fifteen Ways to Make a Cat Love You**
*by Ewen*

begins with…

Feed it fifteen times a day, when it needs you – attend it and stroke it…

and finishes with…

…buy it a personal pillow with its name sewn on, when it dies use a gravestone and plant a tree in its memory.

This list poem format has a lot of potential for children's poetry. Another version might be to write down ten things that they would find in a particular container – a mermaid's purse, a footballer's shoulder bag, a mad scientist's briefcase or the prime minister's glove compartment. Remind them that they should feel happy to take risks with their writing and to think of items that are witty and surprising.

**Ten Things Found in Beckham's Shoulder Bag**
(written when Becks was still at Man U!)
*by Nico*

1. Socks.
2. £1,000,000 in cash.
3. Christmas card from Santa.
4. Spare net in case he breaks the first.
5. Scissors for different hair cuts, although he doesn't need them at the moment.
6. TV camera, if he's not on TV he can film himself!
7. All his team-mates' names in case he forgets.
8. Alec's phone number.
9. Lucky ball for free kicks.
10. Goalkeeper's gloves in case he's needed.

Stella listed the items that might be found in a model's handbag. By playing around with her ideas she was able to turn them into a poem using rhyming couplets:

**A Model's Handbag**
*by Stella*

In a model's handbag you might find
The reddest lipstick (the very best kind).
The smelliest perfume that would make you faint,
Eyeshadow that sticks to you like paint.

Blush that makes you look like you've run a race,
A mirror to compliment your face.
An expensive pot of fine face cream
(ooey, gooey and very green).

Mascara to give you fine black lashes,
Powder that gives you awful rashes.
Some Australian cigarettes (very rare)
And spray for last-minute spraying of hair.

● Poems for two voices

**The Password**
*by Brian Moses*
(Extract)

What's the password?
I don't know.
You can't come in.
Who says so?

I say so.
You and whose army?
Tell me the password.
You must be barmy!

Just tell it me now.
What if I don't?
I'll have to fight you.
Oh no you won't.

What's the password?
I've forgotten.
Tell me the password.
You're just being rotten.

Tell me the password,
Tell it to me.
Tell you the password?
Oh what can it be?

Talk about writing a poem for two or more voices.

Ask children to think of a situation involving a conflict of some kind as in *The Password*. The poem doesn't have to rhyme, but it should have a rhythm so that it sounds good when it is read aloud. Maybe the piece is about someone wanting to do something that a friend doesn't want to do. Maybe the voices echo each other as in the following piece.

**Barry and His Head Teacher**
*by Brian Moses*

Barry went home to his Mum and said...
(Barry's Head Teacher telephoned his wife and said...)
I can't do anything right at school,
(I can't stand another day at this school,)
The teacher told me off and when I asked why,
(This lad called Barry is driving us wild.)
He sent me to the Head Teacher who sat me down,
(I had him in my office all afternoon.)
and made me do nothing till the others went home.
(It was such a relief when I could let him go.)

Alternatively you could get the children to try writing a poem based on a telephone conversation:

*Hi, it's me, I'm on my mobile phone, thought I'd give you a call to say I'm coming back home.*

*Well it's about time too, where have you been? You could have called me earlier, you're so mean.*

After the first drafts of these poems are completed, ask your writers to share their work and perform the poems in pairs. Remind children that an audience will really want to hear the differences between the voices. Think how these can be accentuated.

## • Dreams

Ask the children to imagine that an animal or an object could dream. What might an animal dream about? Perhaps a cat would dream of being a superhero, or a snail would dream of being an Olympic sprinter. Dreams, as we know, can be really weird so this is an invitation for children to really stretch their imaginations. What if a toothbrush could dream?

**My Toothbrush Dreams...**
*by Year 5 Writers, St. James' CE School, Tunbridge Wells*

My toothbrush dreams of being a superstar in Hollywood
and going to the Big Apple.
It dreams of climbing the Eiffel Tower or bungee jumping
down the White Cliffs of Dover.
My toothbrush dreams of flying away
and eating a giant doughnut,
of meeting all the pop stars like Take That.
My toothbrush dreams of going on Celebrity Ready Steady
Cook and being the celebrity,
or winning all the gold medals in the Olympic Games.

*continued...*

My toothbrush dreams of conquering the world
and all must obey him
or being as strong as Arnold Schwarzenegger
or being the superhero Supertoothbrush, just like Superman.
My toothbrush dreams of being invincible
and fighting all the baddies
of eating all the lovely food in the world and not getting fat.
My toothbrush dreams...

Children can easily come up with all kinds of strange ideas. Here's a poem that had a great ending.

**A Zero Dreams of Being a Hero**
*by Jacob*
. . .
What a day, if that could happen
And what a life he could have led.
But Zero couldn't be a hero
Because he couldn't get out of bed!

* Strange hobbies

Ask children to invent strange hobbies for themselves. Nothing ordinary, for example:

- *Making sculptures with fruit peel;*
- *Keeping pet parasites;*
- *Worshipping turnips;*
- *Juggling with rice;*
- *Collecting bricks.*

Now ask them to take this odd hobby and think of all that it would entail. They should try to stretch the idea as far as they can.

**Keeping Cucumbers**
*by Alexis*

Keeping pet cucumbers isn't easy,
they have to eat pepper and make you wheezy.
They demand a walk once a day,
they bite if you don't obey.

Keeping pet cucumbers isn't easy,
they'll only live in a cage that smells cheesy.
They eat all your hair,
they give you a scare,
no, keeping pet cucumbers isn't easy.

**Climbing**
*by Rachel*

On Wednesday I go wall climbing
You can climb right to the top,
You can even go blindfolded!
Or you can boulder down low
Right round the room.
Use chalk to grip.
It will help you.
You should try
Climbing
Too.

• A special place

Discuss with your group of children the idea of a special or secret place where they would like to go to escape when life gets too boring, or too exciting, or too scary, or too difficult. Children will suggest a wealth of places – attics, caves, tree houses, garden sheds, cupboards, desert islands – and these can become a focus for writing. Get them to think about how to make their secret place sound inviting to others.

**My Special Place**
*by Louise*

My special place is in the bathroom,
climb the stairs,
open the door,
then I'm in the bathroom.
I feel happy on the outside,
sad on the inside.
I hear my family
banging on the doors,
shouting at me.
Louise, if you do not open this door,
I'll kick it down.
As they shout this
I'm thinking in my head, Yeah, right.
I let them get angry
while I'm enjoying my magazines.
As they carry on shouting
I start to feel happy, inside and out.
In my head I'm thinking,
revenge, sweet, sweet revenge.

● Your worst journey

Ask the question, what was your worst journey?

It could be a seemingly endless plane flight or car journey. For Brian, as a child, it was the mile he had to walk across town with his mum to reach the dreaded dentist! Roger once got stuck in a car in a blizzard. It was very cold and very frightening.

Once a journey has been decided upon, get the children to make a list of where the journey began, several points along the way and where it ended. They should also list all the aspects of the journey which made it 'the worst'. Discourage everyone from writing about too much 'throwing up'. It doesn't make for terribly pleasant reading and, anyway, we've all been on those kind of trips.

(Many boys have a predilection for poo and fart jokes, as well as extreme violence. We usually explain that although there's nothing wrong with this, it is too easy a route for clever children to take. Poo jokes can guarantee a laugh – but, as able writers, we are looking for something a bit cleverer than this. This did backfire on Roger once, though, when he had lots of work handed in about diarrhoea – and they all spelled it right. Very clever!)

**My Worst Journey**
*by Christopher*

Oh mum, I really don't want to go!
*You're going and that's that!!!*
Great, you can always tell with
the that's that business, you've got no choice.
Now I'm in the hearse on the way to the scalpers.
I can see one of my friends
On the pavement,
Bet he's not going where I'm going.
Past Sainsbury's, past the SWEET SHOP!!!
Oh well, I've arrived there now.
I've arrived at the man with the longest
scissors in the galaxy!

● Pirates

Brian once passed a woman and a young boy in the street as the child said, 'Mum, did pirates wear nail varnish?' He immediately wrote this down in the notebook that all writers carry with them at all times. He knew the question would be the start of a poem that would let him look at pirates in a totally different way.

**Pirates Today**
*by Brian Moses*

Pirates today wear nail varnish
and eat after dinner mints,
they visit expensive hairdressers
and highlight their hair with tints.

They like to eat cucumber
sandwiches
and always take delicate bites.
They sip their Earl Grey tea
and enjoy having early nights.

They talcum powder their feet
and apply their suntan lotion.
They struggle to keep their hair
tidy
when blown about on the ocean.

They floss their teeth after meals
and keep their toenails short.
They always speak well of their
mums,
remembering what they've been
taught.

And you'll see them on
TV chat shows
being terribly polite
and certainly never admitting
that they ever got into a fight!

Children always get the point that this poem is a topsy-turvy look at pirates. They know what pirates were 'really' like but they can see it's fun to look at them in a different way. Get them to think of other groups of people – spacemen, politicians, policemen, teachers, traffic wardens – and to write a poem in the style of the above where the second and fourth lines rhyme.

This exercise enables you to teach them about irony – describing a group of people as they are not, and using words which reveal by their opposites how these people really are. It also allows you to help your group work on rhyme. You will be able to steer them away from using words 'just because' they rhyme and instead towards finding words that fit the sense of the poem as well as rhyme. You may want to collect all the ideas the children have first and then, with their help, shape them into a poem with the aid of a rhyming dictionary.

*Politicians never argue,*
*they always admit when they're wrong.*
*They do juggling tricks in the Commons*
*and often break into a song.*

• Teacher for sale

Children become very quickly engaged when you suggest they imagine how interesting it would be to sell the school, the Head Teacher or the caretaker. Or, of course, you!

Get them to look through newspapers and magazines for examples of how advertisements are worded – in particular small ads. Local papers and free sheets are good for this, but national papers are good, too. Pages can be scanned and shown on the whiteboard or read out.

Work through an example with the children before asking them to write their own adverts.

*Example – The school caretaker*
1. *Discuss reasons why they might want to sell the school caretaker.*
2. *In order to sell him or her they won't want to put potential buyers off – so they should make a list of all his good points.*
3. *Discuss what the advert will look like. Will there be a picture?*
4. *Get them to sketch out the advert, remembering to include a price and how to collect the person for sale.*

Then get the children to write similar pieces based on other people they would like to sell. It should be someone they know – nominally, like the school cook or crossing person, or maybe a member of the family like a brother or sister. Before you begin it might be worth explaining that the project is meant to be fun, not a cathartic experience or a chance to rubbish the school or someone you've just had a row with!

Suggest the children write more way-out adverts. How would they sell the country, or the planet Earth? Get them to write an advert as a poem.

# Freestyle writing

Many children, including able writers, find it difficult to actually begin writing: **Blank Page Syndrome** sets in.

This exercise is adapted from an idea by Peter and Ann Sansom (see *Jumpstart* by Cliff Yates, The Poetry Society 1999).

### • Imagine a person

Start this session by asking the children to imagine a person. This must be someone whom they know very well – someone that they know personally. It can be a friend, a member of the family or someone they know at school.

Ask them to think about what that person looks like, to imagine the person in their mind's eye:
- *Is he tall, short, fat, thin?*
- *Is she full of energy or lethargic?*
- *How does he dress? Is she neat and tidy? Does he wear fashionable clothes, or expensive and understated clothes? Does she go for a casual and sporty look?*

Ask them to think about the person's personality:
- *Is he kind, thoughtful, outgoing, crazy, staid, laid back?*
- *Does she get angry easily?*
- *Does he have a hobby?*

Now ask them to think about their relationship with the person:
- *When did they meet and how long have they known each other?*
- *How do they get on?*
- *What sort of things do they do together?*

Each pupil needs paper or a book to write in. Explain that they can write anything at all about that person. Also promise them that no one will see their writing. What they write will be entirely personal and for their eyes only. (There are two reasons for this: first, to encourage them to write freely and, second, to help those children who become very concerned about a teacher's approval of their work – which for some can be very intimidating.)

Also explain that there is a rule that they MUST follow – to remind them you could write this on the board: **Once you begin writing you must not stop.**

Explain that even if they can't think of anything to write they must write something. Even if it's 'I can't think of anything to write.'

When everyone's ready, tell them that they have exactly three minutes to write down as much as they can. Quantity is more important than quality in this exercise; this is stream-of-consciousness brain dumping.

Wait for the second hand to reach the twelve and say 'Ready steady go!' Admonish anyone whose pen is not scribbling away furiously.

After exactly three minutes say, 'Stop!'

Ask if anyone would like to share their writing, but stress that this is purely optional. (Remember that you promised them they could keep their writing private!) Ask them how they could use what they have written: In a story? As part of a poem? Maybe there's something there that could be expanded into a whole poem or a longer piece of prose.

# Getting Moving: Mainly Poems

# People and situations

**Bicycle Betty**
*by Peter*

I see Betty cycling all over Longlevens,
even down dead ends and backstreet lanes.
She always seems to be where I'm walking,
even when I don't expect her.

She never walks,
always cycles place to place,
and is always wearing her pink knitting
wrapped tightly across her face.

She sometimes comes up to me
and speaks in a friendly voice.
She always tells me how far she's travelled
and various other biking tips.

Betty gets very excited when I say,
"That's an impressive distance to travel."
And then her voice rises to a high-pitched laughter,
but she has already gone round the bend.

● Characters from the past

Tell the children about some characters from your past. Ours include an elderly aunt who flapped tea towels at the cows that invaded her garden, an uncle who cleaned every pair of shoes in the house each Sunday morning before lining them up for inspection, another aunt who had a wonderful parrot who swore vigorously and the man up the road who sometimes sat on his roof and pelted us all with stale bread! Invite contributions from the children about characters they know – the awful next-door neighbour, the strange shopkeeper, Dad's dreadful friend, a weird aunt or uncle, the irritating guest at a holiday hotel.

Now ask the children to choose a character (avoiding parents, brothers and sisters, friends, current teachers – these people are too close and this activity works best with a bit of distance between writer and subject). Next, brainstorm for ways to describe these characters. Fill the board with such prompts as:

- *appearance (face, hair, eyes, clothes);*
- *voice;*
- *irritating or favourite sayings;*
- *habits, good and bad;*
- *basic personality traits;*
- *mannerisms;*
- *hobbies;*
- *pets;*
- *home;*
- *friends.*

The children should then write down five things about their chosen character. Give them ten minutes or so to construct a list of points they want to include. From this list there may emerge a first sentence for a piece of prose or the first line of a poem, an 'Aunt Rose flapped tea towels at cows' sort of sentence – a beginning that is likely to intrigue the reader and make her want to find out more about the character. Then get the children to try to place the character in a potentially interesting situation – cleaning the car, riding a bike, coming round for tea, mowing the lawn – and to build up their prose or poetry from there.

In an exercise such as this we are looking for a number of things in the finished writing:

1. An intriguing first line.

2. The ability to **show** rather than **tell** the reader – writing 'Guy is in a grumpy mood' is **telling** the reader; writing 'Guy banged open the classroom door, stomped across the floor, thumped his bag down on the table, sat down heavily and glared round the room', **shows** the same thing.

3. Stretched ideas. So many poems that children write are simply line after line of different ideas. An idea is thought of, written down in one line and then discarded rather than explored. If children take an idea and stretch it over three or four lines, it can be far more interesting. Show them how. For example, instead of:
   *Grandad loves watching television*
   *He drives a blue car*
   *He likes to grow marrows ...*

   Take each line and tell the reader more about the idea:
   *Grandad loves watching television*
   *His favourite programme is The Weakest Link*
   *I think he fancies Anne Robinson...*

4. Good use of simile, metaphor, personification – techniques which the children have used to make their writing more interesting.

5. A satisfying last line. The end of a poem should make the reader smile or laugh or feel sad, or wonder or shiver.

In the poem below and in *Bicycle Betty* above, both writers have highly intriguing endings. Betty's 'already gone round the bend'. And what's in store for Mum?

### The Woman Who Stole My Mum
*by Ellie*

My Mum was stolen in an aircraft!
On a flight from Gatwick to Malta
By Ruth.
Ruth was stuck to my Mum like superglue.
Always at mealtimes,
By the pool,
Even in our hotel room.
They never stopped talking.
Ruth spoke 24-7 about
My son does this and works here and is married to her…
Yawn!
I told my Mum about Ruth trying to steal her.
She didn't listen.
I told my sister. Guess what!
She didn't listen.
At dinner we had the same conversation with Ruth.
Do you behave well at home?
Are you clever at school?
All the same.
On the coach to the airport I felt sick.
Well I wasn't, I pretended.
But it worked!
I got to sit next to Mum.
On the plane to Gatwick
I got to sit next to Mum!
At Gatwick we got Ruth's address.
My Mum and Ruth will go away together
I know it.
And my poor old Mum won't have a clue,
She's stolen property!

**My Grandad**
*by Andrew*

His words are as muddled as a toddler's drawing.
His hair is grey and thin and bald on top
where scabs and bruises lie.
As far back as I can remember
he has never been well.
Death is taking him in the most painful way it can, killing brain cells
one after the other.
Destroying knowledge, the difference between a mug and a jug,
recognition
of what a grandson is, who his grandson is –
who I am.

**Dad's Neighbour**
*by Torty*

The man in the caravan next door nit-picked his way to dad's wits'
end. He was always complaining, the sun was too bright, the wind
was too strong, the grass was too wet, there was never a moment of
peace. When you complained about him, however, his face swelled
up like a beetroot and he exploded into a mass of insults.

**Grandad Tony**
*by Zannia*
(Extract)

Grandad Tony never stops talking.
He is a vicar,
but my dad calls it God Bothering.
My grandad gets angry and wags a finger.
My dad just laughs
and I laugh with him.

It is often best for children to start with someone they know. They can take a mental snapshot of a real person and this can be a springboard for their ideas. If children run out of ideas, remind them that writers often base their characters on a real person but also bring in character traits from others along the way. Characters in books are mostly 'composites'. Remind children that they are writers too and that they can use their imaginations to make their characters more entertaining.

**My Neighbour**
*by Alex*

My neighbour imposes more security measures on her plants than Fort Knox! Her husband only comes out of his shed once a week because he's so busy building new weapons like heat-seeking machetes, bullet-firing sprinklers and – his latest project – robot assassins! Any fox that slinks in doesn't slink out. Their house is a fortress. All because of a £12 bamboo sapling off eBay.

**Aunt Lisa**
*by Harry*

Is Aunt Lisa just a strange girl or is she a ghost in disguise?
The mystic ball inside her room, a bowling ball of glass,
The souls trapped inside who ask to go free,
But Aunt Lisa won't let them go from her grasp.
She hides the monster inside, in a cocoon of skin.
The carefree state she's in is just a disguise
For the strange woman within.
She crafts in wood an ancient script.
You can see the evil dripping out like cobra's venom.
She talks on the phone for years at a time.
Who's on the other end?
Maybe a werewolf on a skateboard drinking monkey blood
through a straw,
Or maybe a vampire riding in Van Helsing's car.
No one knows her true identity. I think she's the queen of demons.

# Phantom figures

**The Ghost of the Forest**
*by Josie*
(Extract)

Lonely old spirit, sad old spook, lies in his oak
for hours on end, waiting, waiting for the moon to ride in.
His shabby clothes cover his scaly body
giving him a look of horrible longing.
His mocking look of sadness stays forever on his face
as he moans to the wind and cries to the stars.

Children find scary things stimulating. Begin by talking about ancient people and their beliefs in gods and goddesses that were linked to aspects of nature – the sun god, moon goddess, gods of the sea and the storm and so on.

Many beliefs were also founded on the idea that spirits, phantom figures, were linked to specific places. Tree worshippers would offer prayers to the spirit of a tree, asking the tree spirit to make it rain if their crops were failing through drought, or to make the sun shine if there had been too much rain. Spirits might also be linked to lakes, streams, valleys, forests, glades. Ancient people must have had some idea in their heads of what such spirits might look like.

## • On ghosts and spirits

Ask children to think of places they have been, places that they can conjure up in their minds:

- *a wood near to where they live;*
- *a stretch of beach;*
- *a mountain stream;*
- *a dense forest;*
- *a lake;*
- *a glacier;*
- *a derelict factory;*
- *a canal through a city;*
- *a volcano.*

Next, ask the children to try to create in words the form and shape of the spirit who might inhabit their chosen place, making sure that there is a sense as to why their phantom figure is linked to the place where it belongs.

Alternatively, if they have problems with finding a place, encourage them to think about what a fire spirit might look like, or the spirit of ice, sun, moon, stars, storm.

When helping your children to read through their first drafts, consider again the five points mentioned in the previous section, *People and situations,* page 31.

**The Fire Spirit**
*by Harley*

The spirit of fire is a burning colossus
making scorched footprints wherever he goes.
His hair is a mass of coiling, writhing fire worms
snapping and biting at everything.
His eyes are just holes in his orange face
staring at everything with keen interest.
His mouth is a cavernous tomb
lined with razor-sharp teeth.
His breath can melt steel,
making an inferno of flames appear and disappear,
reducing everything to embers and ashes.
The torso of the fire spirit is a man's down to the waist
but the rest is flames
making the air shimmer around him.
He floats as quick as light, touching things as he goes.
He causes forest fires and building fires,
punishing the gods for trapping him in fire.

In commenting on this piece of work it would be worth mentioning how Harley has made excellent use of the vocabulary of fire. His first line pulls us into the poem and makes us want to read more, while the last line really makes the reader think about the fire spirit who is so keen to get his own back on the gods. There are still one or two places where the writing is weak – razor-sharp teeth is a cliché, while 'touching things as he goes' is far too vague, and the rhythm needs working on – but for a first effort it is excellent.

In the next piece, Grace puts in a powerful plea on behalf of Mother Earth.

**Earth Song**
*by Grace*

She is the ground, the soil in which we plant our hopes, our lives, our dreams. She is the back that bends under selfish feet, with no support to hold her there, withstanding all the threats and cruelty and pain she is forever to endure. She appears to us in good food, material to hold our houses and build our machinery, flowers to brighten and sweeten a bitter world. Yet how do we repay her? How do we return what is given? Machinery is used to rake and scar her good earth, poison her and make waste of her food. Her surface is used as a battlefield to be trampled with blood and bodies till she aches and groans with sadness and fatigue. And the creatures her maker created, that ruin her surface, are shunned, wrecked with hunger and illness because of their race or disabilities. Yet, through all of this devastation, all this weeping and grinding of teeth, she is still able to pull herself up, break the surface of sadness and mend the wounds. She makes light on dark times, she is a voice calling out in the wilderness, calling, calling her children home. Her name is Mother Earth.

# Take an idea and s-t-r-e-t-c-h it

**Doris, the Death-Defying Dormouse**
*by Poppy*

Doris, my dormouse, may not have one hundred arms,
But
She does have wings of steel that reflect laser
and anti-gravity light-as-a-feather paws.
She does have teeth as sharp as our Head Teacher's stare
and a super-smeller nose that can smell a bug in America.
She does have eyes with sonar power
and a tail that can change the way of the wind.
She does have a memory that never forgets
and can cook the best type of cookie.
She does have the strength to swim round the world
and could carry me twice around China.
She does have a cage that will keep her at bay
and now she's asleep in her pile of sawdust.

*What happens when you take an idea and stretch it?*

## • Similes and super creatures

Begin with similes. Check that children know what a simile is and then ask them to write down as many similes as they can think of. After a few minutes go through the lists. Many children will have written down examples of common similes that they will have come across in books and at home – as black as ink, as cold as ice, as good as gold, as slow as a snail, as white as a sheet, as quiet as a mouse. Now point out how inaccurate some of these similes are in today's world. How many sheets are white these days? Has anyone lived in a house where there are mice – they certainly aren't quiet, especially at night if they live in the loft!

Discuss with the children how it is the writer's task to reject similes that are tired or overused and to look for fresh ways of making comparisons. Now ask them to take a well-used simile and to stretch it till it says something new; for example, 'as slow as a snail' could become 'as slow as a snail pushing a brick'. Make something even taller by stretching it from 'as tall as a giraffe' to 'as tall as a giraffe on stilts'. Then invite other comparisons. You could encourage the group by suggesting:

- *As weird as a dandelion clock saying tick tock.*
- *As slow as a farmer pushing his tractor up a steep hill.*
- *As sleepy as Sleeping Beauty waiting for a handsome Prince.*
- *As unhappy as a shoe being worn by a smelly foot.*

Children can then be encouraged to use such ideas in a poem which builds on one stretched simile after another.

This exercise involves taking an ordinary creature and turning it into a super creature. Ask the children to decide on a creature – a pet, zoo animal, farm animal, fish, bird, insect. Once this has been decided, ask them to find an adjective to describe their creature. Some alliteration could be effective here – my crazy crocodile, magnificent maggot, fantastic frog...

Start with a class poem on the board, which will then act as a guide for those who wish to follow it. Always make clear, however, that should anyone wish to adapt the model and take it off in another direction, then this is to be encouraged.

Now get the children to think of a first line, perhaps to do with the creature's size:
- *My terrifying tortoise is as heavy as a hippo holding weights.*

Now ask them about its strength and speed:
- *It is as strong as Hercules lifting the Eiffel Tower.*
- *And as fast as Shaun Wright-Phillips with rocket boosters.*

How noisy is it?

- *It is as noisy as a volcano erupting into a microphone....*

Ask the children to carry on adding to their poems by thinking about what and how much the creature eats and drinks, what its special characteristics are – very sharp claws, colourful wings, a long furry tail, etc. Is it fierce or friendly? Does it need protection – and if so from what – or does it protect you?

In the following examples, imaginations have certainly been stretched.

**My Cousin's Gerbil**
*by Max*

When my cousin talks about his gerbil, he says that:

Its tail is like a huge viper that creeps through the sand and dirt.
It is as black as the night,
as black as the wet tyres of the HGV from Hell.
Its soft and deep fur is often covered with dirt,
as it burrows long, deep tunnels to faraway worlds.
He says it often goes mountain climbing and pot-holing.
It does abseiling and scuba diving,
It does llama trekking and bare-back riding.
Its cage is the size of the NEC in Birmingham but it often escapes
to find new adventures in America or Asia.
It likes to eat curry and pizza (vegetables only),
not the usual diet for a rodent.
After eating, it runs for miles, getting faster and faster,
like a super-pigeon with rocket blasters.
My cousin goes on for hours about this beast,
telling of its great and marvellous feats.

And I don't believe a word of it.

But you should see my rabbit...

**The Stupid Dumb Slug**
*by Samantha*

This stupid slug thinks he can beat Carol Vorderman in a maths quiz.
He reckons he could win one million on Who Wants to be a Millionaire.
He says he could rule Broadway while playing ping pong,
Then boasts that he can beat a car in speedway
and kill everyone in fighting.
He thinks that he's as big as a T. Rex in a museum
and as elegant as a dancer.
He says he knows the meaning to every word in the English
Dictionary.
His job, he thinks, should be a lawyer, but he'd rather be an MP.
He wants to be the new Superman
and lift the heaviest weights.
His favourite shop is Gap while he still likes Gucci.
He said he passed his driving test first time when he was seven.
(Well, it was at Legoland.)
He says he's going to be the new Pavarotti while dancing the can-can.
He says he has the body for the catwalk.
He's definitely dreaming,
That stupid dumb slug.

If you'd like to follow up this exercise, take a look at the poems of Ted Hughes in his book **Moon-Whales** (Faber & Faber). In this collection your able writers will be particularly interested in **The Snail of the Moon** (which has a wail...as though something had punctured him), **Moon-Heads** (... shining like lamps and light as balloons), and **Moon-Witches** (...looking exactly like cockroaches). These poems by this former Poet Laureate could provide your group with more models and further inspiration for imagination-stretching pieces about space creatures. Encourage them to write about the Jaguar of Jupiter, the Slithering Snakes of Saturn, the Vole of Venus and so on. This time in their poems, as well as describing the creatures in colourful language, suggest that the children think about how these creatures interact with others. Do the Monkeys of Mercury visit the Pythons of Pluto or fight with the Newts of Neptune?

Alternatively, bring children back down to Earth and find nasty creatures in the local environment – the Ogre of Oswestry, the Terrifying Troll of Tring or the Dreadful Dragon of Dorchester.

*The Dreadful Dragon of Dorchester*
*Was as plump as an old oak and tall as a willow.*
*His footstep was an earthquake,*
*A mountain was his pillow.*

# Making the familiar scary

*by Year 5 Writers, Queen Eleanor Junior School, Guildford*

I saw the piano lid gently rise without a hand to lift it.
I discovered that the pictures on the wall were peeling off.
I felt the sweep of a piece of paper as if somebody very gently touched me on the shoulder.
I heard the clock ticking, ticking, ticking and then nothing.
I touched the portrait of Queen Elizabeth, her eyes flared and gazed at me.
I noticed a flash from the projector next to me.
I touched the radiator as a horrible cold tingle climbed up my fingertips.
I stared at the light switches flicking up and down but they didn't come on.
I found writing on the blackboard that wasn't there before.
I felt warm breath down my back...

● Writing a performance piece

Talk about the way that film directors use hand-held cameras to film the scary bits in their films and discuss what might be the reason for using this sort of camera rather than a camera mounted on a tripod.

Hand-held cameras bring the actors right into the centre of the action. As you watch the scary parts, you are that person walking up the stairs of a spooky house, you are that person looking into the different rooms then reaching the one room at the end of the corridor where you realise that something awful must have happened or is about to happen…

Explain to the children that they are about to create a similar effect but with words. They should imagine that they have returned to their school at midnight. All the doors are open and so they go in. The lights aren't working but there is enough moonlight for them to see the shapes around them. They make their way carefully to their classroom.

Ask the children to now think of ways in which they can turn their familiar classroom into something strange and scary. But it's not going to be as easy as they might think because there is an important rule – they may not import any ghosts, vampires, werewolves, disembodied arms, feet, heads or pools of blood! In fact they must use only what would normally be found in the room: furniture, equipment, books, papers, artwork, cupboards and so on.

Ask them to begin each sentence with the word 'I'. This has the effect of bringing a real person into the centre of the action: *I saw, I found, I heard, I noticed, I discovered, I came across, I felt, I smelt, I noticed, I touched*. It also has the effect of giving the piece a rhythm and a chant-like quality.

Point out that this is not a story, rather a series of separate observations that can be linked together to make a performance piece or chant. The first sentence could be something like:

*I heard the globe spin without the touch of a finger.*

It is important that the children do not turn what they are writing into a story at this point, as the second stage of the exercise is to rearrange the observations so that they read from the least spooky line through to the most scary, so ending with that moment when you realise that you are not alone in the room because... 'a hand grips my shoulder'! (If you shout out this line it makes everyone jump.)

The classroom example, which begins 'I saw the piano lid gently rise', at the start of this section, is a composite poem made up of lines from a number of pieces and at this stage children need to give some thought as to how this could be performed.

As this piece isn't one with a regular rhyme or rhythm, the effects should concentrate more on heightening the spooky factor. As the teacher, you might want to use props to heighten the atmosphere. Brian often uses an instrument called a spring drum with his spooky poems. This is simply a tube with one end covered by a taut drum skin. Passing through the centre of the drum skin and attached to it is a length of spring. When shaken, the spring vibrates, the vibrations are picked up by the drum skin and are then amplified in the tube giving rather wonderful spooky/stormy effects. (These instruments can be obtained from music catalogues or simply do an internet search for spring drum to find a supplier.)

The funereal beat of a drum might also provide an effective backing to a piece such as this, the low notes on a piano with the loud pedal pushed down or different sound effects from the percussion trolley for each line. Anyone with keyboard and/or computer skills may be able to compose a spooky backing track to which the poem could be read.

It is important to remember too that the voice is also an effective 'instrument' in an exercise like this. It isn't sufficient for the piece to simply be read in a monotone. The voice must sound frightened or alarmed. Sometimes the lines may be best spoken fast with a touch of panic in the voice. At other times they could be slowed down. Variations in pitch will help to conjure the spooky atmosphere. Get the children to whisper and then to YELL, to make their voices sound menacing or frightened.

Finally, if you have access to a video camera, you could film the piece. Don't worry about returning to the classroom at midnight! Just wait for a dull day, turn off the lights, draw down the blinds and film in the gloom.

The poem, with any instrumental additions or sound effects, can then become the soundtrack to the video.

This idea can also be transferred to the school grounds. Using the same method, encourage the children to turn the familiar sights into something spooky:

*I looked along the winding footpath – was it leading to danger?*
*I felt the wind suddenly turn icy and the cold pinch my skin.*
*I saw a feather fall from nowhere and stab the ground.*
*I heard a crack – the roots of the trees were snaking towards me.*

Ask the children to make notes of what is around them. What do they hear, see, smell, taste, feel? Remind them that they're looking for things that will later be useful for a piece of writing that will scare their friends:
- *the school gate creaks;*
- *leaves rustle – something is moving;*
- *a light is on in the school;*
- *the school flag is moving – but there's no wind;*
- *ivy covers the ground, ready to tangle around my feet;*
- *metal railings are cold and sharp;*
- *church bells ring in the far distance;*
- *there are grey shadows and there are darker shadows.*

Then ask the children to use these small, detailed observations to write a scary story. Set the scene: *It's midnight at the school gates*. Ask the children to use their notes and what they've learned about how to make the familiar strange, to think again about what they would hear, see, smell, feel, taste in the middle of the night.

Encourage them to use short sentences, which will heighten the scary feeling, particularly when read aloud, as in Bryony's piece below. Her line about the railings is very effective as is the repetition of the word 'darkness'.

**Who's There?**
*by Bryony*

Footsteps, behind me, as I turn down the street to the school. Louder, louder, not mine, whose? I quicken my pace but they're still there. I want to turn, too scared. I hear whispers that seem to hiss, "Aren't you going to look at us, turn to see us?" I stand petrified and gather courage to turn. I see nothing, only trees. I keep walking.

I open the school gate and hear leaves rustle. The railings behind me make a ringing noise as if a stick is being dragged over them. I feel a cold chill on my cheek. It feels like a cold finger stroking my face. "You've arrived," I seem to hear. My mind tries to banish thoughts. It's just the wind, I say to myself, but I'm not so sure.

The fence is holding back darkness, darkness that wants me, darkness that creeps behind me. I rush towards the entrance and slip inside. I didn't think about the door being open, I just went in.

# I've forgotten something!

## • Revealing a cache of memories

We all have a cache of memories in our heads that we dip into from time to time when we tell anecdotes about places we've been and people we've encountered. Explain to the children that writers, like them, frequently use these memories as a basis for a story or a poem. And searching back through the years can reveal a half-forgotten memory that might be suitable to use in a story or poem which they might be struggling with. These little snippets about people, times or places can often be all that's needed to bring the past into the present and bring the writing to life.

Remind children how they often find memories unexpectedly floating to the surface of their minds. Often, a particular smell or a sound, like a piece of music, acts as a trigger for the memory and you know instantly why you've thought of the past. On other occasions it is difficult to tell what made you remember.

People often say they are no good at remembering faces but have a very good memory for places and things that they've done there, particularly when they've had a good time, like a holiday or a special occasion treat. Get the children to think about what they remember and why. What makes something memorable? Why is this? Are pleasant memories always more powerful than unpleasant ones? Or does it depend on the sort of person we are? What do we do to try to forget things we really don't want to remember?

The point of this is to prepare the children to write about a series of memories, but to imagine that it is forty years in the future and they are looking back on their childhoods. Ask them to write their poem in the form of a letter written to a friend whom they have lost touch with. They should try to bring in as much detail as possible. Perhaps they will be recalling their schooldays, or a special holiday, or playing in the street, or in the woods, or on the beach; or the poem could just gossip about friends and acquaintances.

The poem shouldn't rhyme but it could use repetition to give it a structure, as in the poem below, where Sophie brings in the line 'Have you forgotten?' at various times. This has the effect of stitching the piece together and aiding the rhythmic flow.

### Have You Forgotten?
*by Sophie*

Hello,
Have you forgotten us, and our childish ways?
Have you forgotten the way we used to gossip and giggle
Like squirmy chimpanzees,
About boys and make-up,
And important things?
Have you forgotten, the way we stuck together,
Through thick and thin, no matter what.
That time, by the beach,
When we screamed and danced,
To our own pretend beat,
As the others snickered and stared.
Have you forgotten, the made-up things
We used to do,
Like painting the walls
With nail varnish,
And drawing with lipstick
On the new cream carpets?
Have you forgotten our pretend games
The ones in parallel universes
Where we could fly,
Touch the sky
And glow green at night?
Everyone else thought we were mad
But still we stuck together.
Have you forgotten, the way it all stopped
A single mistake
A single idiotic sentence
That broke it all up.
Our friendship was like the Empire State
Tall with all its glory
But it was broken
By a single crumbling brick.
Then it all collapsed
We drifted apart
And it all stopped
Suddenly, like a plane crash.

*continued...*

Have you forgotten, the ended laughter.
The secret hope, we would be just like we were
Best friends
Have you forgotten me?
Are you trying to forget me
And the way we were?
But you can't erase it
It's more than just mindless scribble,
It was us.
We were more than childish playmates
We were truly best friends
Until that day.
It could never come back though
It was something special
And now it's gone forever.
Do you remember, the first confirmation of my diagnosis,
and how you said:
We won't change,
We won't break,
It doesn't matter,
So, are you now, the betrayal teacher,
The thief of hearts,
The winning contestant in the contest of deception,
Or.....do you truly remember?

# Place names

**Kirk Deighton**
*by Brian Moses*

Kirk Deighton?
That can't be the name of a place!
Sounds more like the name
of a superhero, a secret agent,
someone to swoon over.
Kirk Deighton,
suave, sophisticated,
a gold-plated gun in a shoulder holster,
hairy chest, bullet proof vest.
The kind of guy that girls adore,
a secret spy on a dangerous mission
somewhere off the A1, South Yorkshire.

Places and place names – street names, shop signs, villages, rivers, lakes etc – provide a great source of ideas for the writer. The Carpet Showroom can become the Car Pet Showroom or places can become people as with the village Brian found in Yorkshire called Kirk Deighton.

● What's in a name?

Ask the children to look in an atlas to discover places with strange names both in the UK and abroad. In Australia there's Lake Disappointment and the Simpson Desert. Around the world there's Yellowknife, Great Sugar Loaf, Cape Fear, Death Valley and Christmas Island. In the UK there's Frog Street, Labour-in-vain Hill, Dull, Barking, Muck, Bath, Cheddar, Lower Slaughter and everyone's favourite, Pratt's Bottom!

Once lists have been compiled, talk about the names. Identify those that best lend themselves to use in a poem. Then ask the children to look at these places in a different way. Begin by asking questions. *In Frog Street, do they eat their burgers with flies not fries?* Encourage them away from the obvious, like *Do they only eat turkey in Turkey?* Much better would be to ask *Do they ever eat chicken in Turkey? Can you fish for red snapper or grey mullet in the Black Sea? Does the chemist sell a lot of sleeping tablets on Wake Island?*

**The Wash**
*by Siobhan*

Is everything wet in the Wash?
Or is everything always spotless?
Does anything ever get dirty?

Can you stink in the Wash or
Do you have to smell like roses?

Can you have messy rooms or
Will you get told off if you have
even a speck of dust?

Is everything always
immaculate in the Wash?
Or is it littered
like London?

**Staple Hill**
*by Zoe*

If you go up Staple Hill
I can warn you you'll never come back down,
They'll pin your smile upside down
and your face will become a frown!

Your feet will be tied down tight
And your arms and legs will link,
Or maybe they'll grasp you close,
What on earth do you think?

You can allow the children a fair bit of poetic licence with the pronunciation of names. Greenwich turns into Green Witch, an environmentally friendly witch. In Alabama, Mobile is not pronounced like the phone – but that doesn't matter!

**Mobile**
*by Elouise*

Do the phones always need charging in Mobile?
Do they always ring off the hook?
Do people walk around chatting
or just reading the directory book?

Next encourage the children to try using place names in a slightly different way. This time ask them to write as if the place itself was speaking. They might then boast about their powers, beauty, charm, peacefulness or mischievousness, as in the poems below.

**Mount Everest**
*by Cameron*

I am Mount Everest,
Very much the cleverest
Mountain in the world.
I send climbers to their doom
And rescuers to their tomb.
I am a silent and majestic mountain,
All who challenge my wrath are condemned to stumble upon
    my path of death.
My mighty peaks and frozen glaciers are the bane of every
    climber.
None can scale my frozen greatness,
All who try will fail,
For I am Mount Everest,
Surely the cleverest
Mountain of them all.

**Lake Victoria**
*by Lok*

I am Lake Victoria,
wrapped in royal gowns of blue.
Sunlight shines upon me and only shines upon me.
With my parasol of bubbles I shield the creatures inside me.
I am Lake Victoria.

**Mount Etna**
*by Joseph*

I am Mount Etna,
I am tall and wide.
I can see over Europe,
I can see over the sea.
Over the Mediterranean Sea
is Africa, hot and poor.

I may be smaller than Mont Blanc
But I'm bigger than Vesuvius
My cousin in the north.
I may be an island
but that doesn't change my size.
The island I'm on is tiny
I can cover the whole place up.
I may be small to other mountains
but I am brave inside.
Beware Mount Etna.

Once the children understand that a different approach is what gets writers noticed, and makes readers want to read what they've written, your able writers will be keen to come up with ideas themselves, rather than use those that are handed out to them. Give them an open-ended activity and this will just happen.

# Positives from negatives

**The Alley**
*by Ellie*

The alleyway glowered like a moon without its shine.
The wall groaned with graffiti.
Broken glass scattered across the floor.
And behind the bin a cat looked up at me with despair in its eyes.
But there in the corner a pearl white moth
fluttered past the beaten fence and up to the stars.

• Making a silk purse

This exercise encourages children to find good in bad, to take positive thoughts from negative input, as in these two lines from Brian's poem, Spring in the City:

> *...And a single primrose shows its head*
> *at the dump,*
> *like a lucky charm.*

Brian also remembers when he was a teacher and his class visited the local water-treatment works. He vividly remembers one boy pointing out, amidst all the sludge, a small piece of silver foil reflecting the sun.

Talk to your children about places they have visited that at first sight seemed ugly or unpleasant. Focus on places that children know in their own locality – a derelict house or garden, litter-strewn alleyway, polluted beach, rubbish tip, etc. Inevitably someone will mention public toilets and you will need to consider whether the writer is capable of dealing with this subject in a sensible manner! Warn about going OTT!

To encourage them to take a different slant on this, ask the children if they have memories of places they have visited on holiday that were not as attractive as they had been led to believe. We've all heard about the hotel complex that was actually still a building site and most of us have come across the picnic site spoiled by litter, the restaurant yard filled with overflowing dustbins or the smelly drains in a city street.

It's a good idea to begin with a brainstorming session, getting the children to go through the senses and listing all the nasty sights, sounds, smells etc. Ask them to take a mental snapshot of the place they want to write about and to hold it in their heads. How does the place make them feel?

Then suggest that they start to bring their ideas together in a piece of prose or poetry. Once they have described the place and the way it makes them feel, ask them to think very hard about something beautiful or amazing that transforms this horrid place. This should then be used in the last line of their written piece. If they really cannot think of something 'real' then you will need to encourage poetic licence – they must find something that transforms this sow's ear into a silk purse.

**The Quarry**
*by Duncan*

Beyond the road, beyond the wood,
Lies the old quarry pit.
Outcrops of rock leaning in
Over the bed of nettles.
Far, far, far down there
Where only the experts venture,
A short burst of movement,
And again, just over there,
A rat darts under the metal.
Huge girders twined and twisted
Together reaching for the sky.
A smell of decaying metal
Seems to haunt this silent place.
At the other side of this hole,
A trickle of fresh running water
Splashes into the old quarry,
Bringing life into this dead place.

## About Noah's Ark

So what was it really like, sailing with Noah on the Ark?

**The Giraffe's Dream**
*by Daniel*

I really wish that there was a tree full of leaves in here. Every time I go to sleep (which is not very often), I dream of a lost island full of giraffes, food and water. Just that is what I want more than anything else in the world right now.

For this piece of work we'll be asking the children to discuss the problems faced by those on board Noah's Ark. Geraldine McCaughrean, in her children's book *Not the End of the World*, writes about life on board the Ark, a vessel where humans and animals were closeted together for months. Apart from the smell and the practical reality of getting rid of all that animal waste, there would have been other problems too, such as keeping the lions and antelopes apart. Not to mention having enough food on board for both the lions and antelopes to eat.

At the start of the voyage, when the flood waters rose, there would have been hundreds of people swimming in the water or paddling makeshift boats. They would all be clamouring to be taken on board the Ark. If you had been Noah could you have refused them?

## • Don't miss the boat!

Ask the children how they would have felt being Noah and begin to identify the kind of problems he and the animals might have had. Write their suggestions on the board:

- loss of habitat;
- fear of drowning;
- ghastly smells;
- overcrowding;
- shortage of food;
- fighting;
- diseases;
- boredom;
- temptation;
- supplies of fresh water.

Now ask the children to choose creatures they might like to be. Remind them that there would have been birds, fish, insects, jungle creatures, farm animals and so on. Make a list of all these creatures on the board. If they haven't been mentioned already, drop some more contentious creatures into the mix such as crocodiles, sloths, wasps, rats, skunks, weevils, stick insects or vultures, for example.

Now ask the children to write from the point of view of one of these creatures, cooped up on the Ark. Ask them how it might feel. Do they have any complaints? What are their hopes, wishes, fears or dreams? They might also involve one or two other creatures in the piece of writing. The lion could be fantasising about catching and eating one of the juicy piglets. The ants might be complaining about being too close to the anteaters. And the skunk might be upset that none of the other animals wants to be his friend. Do allow considerable poetic licence!

### Shark
*by Hannah*

It is the most annoying thing when the goldfish sniggers in the corner. You've been on this boat for nearly 30 weeks and you're the only animal with sense. There's always one monkey with tricks up his sleeve or the odd elephant blowing at your tank. Well, I've had enough of it!

### Monkey
*by Ellie*

Being on this ark is really tough. I haven't swung on anything, I haven't messed about and I certainly haven't been silly or stupid. For a monkey I think I have done well not to annoy any of the other animals... I am so fed up. I really do want to trick someone. Oh, I promised I would be good and sensible and if I don't keep my promise Noah will kick me off the boat.
But it's so tempting.

### Army Ant
*by Ben*

There were two of us, the queen and I. After a month there are now more than a thousand of us. Noah has provided us with leaves and twigs and told us to be peaceful. This has not been successful. The mole trod on ten of us and then we took it in little pieces to the queen. Noah was not happy, so he decided not to open the door of our chamber. We ate the door. The elephants were rocking the boat so we bit their legs. They rocked the boat some more. The lizard ate dozens of our eggs so we ate its wife. Vengeance is sweet!

If you would like to pursue this idea further, there are lots of examples in both fiction and poetry and an internet search should give you plenty of material to use. Roger McGough, in *The Way Things Are*, has a sequence of poems based on this idea called *Bad Day at the Ark* which begins – On the eleventh morning Japhet burst into the cabin: 'Dreadful news everybody, the tigers have eaten the bambanolas!'

You might discuss with the children animals who may not have made the trip.

**Don't Miss the Boat**
*Roger Stevens*

The Woebegoing cried big fat tears
as the animals entered the Ark.
He'd been packing his case for thirteen years,
at first for a bit of a lark.
But now, as the animals boarded the ship,
he sat on the bank and bit his lip.

For thirteen years he'd searched the land
looking for a mate.
For thirteen years he'd sifted sand,
but now it was too late.
He rang his bell,

sung

a farewell song
and the Woebegoing
was the Woebegone.

# Creature encounters

**Kitten**

*by Naomi*

Excited and hyper I bound across the lawn,
I see her for the first time, my kitten, alone,
the trauma from her past still jolts in her eyes.
Holding her softly I walk on ahead.
Slowly I lower her into the box,
her eyes are alive, a new future ahead.
But suddenly a new fear dawns on her face.
Spying a gap she jumps to her feet,
squeezing through, my tiny cat shoots out,
charging across the lawn to another place.
Caught by a woman, put back in our box,
she falls asleep soundly while forms are filled out,
ready for the long journey home
and to a place in my heart.

• Springboard for a story

Children, we know, are attracted to animals of all kinds and encounters with animals, whether they be one-off experiences, such as meeting a bear in a zoo, or on a trail in the Rockies, or the many events that happen during the course of a pet's life; all are a great source of ideas. Many poets and writers of children's fiction look back to animal encounters or remember animals they have known and use these recollections as the springboard for a story.

Tell the children to think of one particular time when they encountered an animal, or to think of a particular episode with a pet, and ask them to recollect how they felt at the time. Encourage them to share their experiences with the class. Then ask the children to write the experiences down as the beginning of a poem.

Most memories will be happy or funny but children will often want to write about the loss of a pet. Suggest that, in their writing, they try to put across their feelings so that others might empathise with what they experienced. And they could ask themselves the question – *Did the encounter change them in some way?*

The five points outlined in *People and Situations* on page 33 may be useful here. In the example at the start of this section, Naomi has written a first line that really draws us into the poem. By writing in the present tense she shows us the experience – it's actually happening rather than being reported and her final line can't fail to touch anyone who has ever fallen in love with a pet. Parts of the poem have a lovely rhythm and sound too: *she falls asleep soundly while forms are filled out.*

The following poem is quite adult in its content, but it may be useful in drawing out memories that have been sidelined. An able writers' group of Year 5 and Year 6s should be capable of listening to the poem and then digging deep into their own memories for encounters with animals that have affected them in some way. A discussion with them might revolve around whether we *should* trap mice or kill slugs, wasps, flies and other irritants. It could produce some interesting and heartfelt poems.

**Mouse**
*by Brian Moses*

The mouse was cold,
nosed its way into our house.
We heard it at night,
a flitter-flutter over our heads.
A bird in the loft, we thought at first,
but investigations showed nothing,
and still we heard
the same slippery scamperings.

"It wouldn't be a mouse," I said,
"Old houses get mice, ours is new."
But it was.
We baulked at poison, laid down
a trap instead.

*continued...*

The first morning nothing.
The second, trap sprung, cheese gone,
no mouse.
Third morning I found it,
still alive, terrified,
trapped by a useless back leg.

It was later too,
I'd avoided looking that morning,
washed, drank tea, read the paper
and all the while the mouse had been there,
curled up with its pain.

In the garden I placed mouse and trap
on the ground,
grabbed a brick and with eyes turned away,
hammered it down.

The remains I buried along with the trap.

And Heaven knows why I thought of it today,
not just the manner of its death
but its terror and its pain.

It was years back, I know,
but memory keeps the mouse alive
over decades of dying.

# Amazing facts about animals

**Swifts**
*by Sam*

Swifts sleep on the wing,
now that's an amazing thing.
Imagine if you were sleeping while you were at school,
you'd be bumping into each and every wall.
You'd probably go to maths when you had P.E.
And go to the wrong toilets when you needed a wee!
But swifts it seems can sleep on the wing
without bumping into a thing.
I find that very hard to believe.

● Outlandish but true

In this activity we ask the children to consider some amazing facts about animals and turn them into a poem. The children can look for some facts to kick-start their poems in the library or on the internet. Or you could use a few of the facts below, all of which are, amazingly, true. Begin by writing some of them on the board.

- *Elephants can't jump.*
- *Camels are born wrestlers.*
- *A hippo can run faster than a man.*
- *Hummingbirds can fly backwards.*
- *Dolphins sleep with one eye open.*
- *Cats cannot taste sweet things.*
- *Earthworms can pull ten times their own weight.*
- *Butterflies taste with their back feet.*
- *Dogs can't see all colours.*
- *The silk-worm moth has eleven brains.*
- *There is an eye on the tip of each arm of a starfish.*
- *An ant can lift 50 times its own body weight.*
- *A caterpillar has 4000 muscles.*

Begin with one fact and ask the children to consider its implications. We are brainstorming here, to gather material for a poem.

For example – **The silk-worm moth has eleven brains**.

So can it multi-task? Can it do homework, play a computer game, check its bank statement and watch TV all at the same time? Could it be a successful candidate for *Mastermind*? Could it write a novel while painting a picture?

**A Male Sea Horse Can Have Children**
*by V.*

Just think of the pain
of a male sea horse having kids,
going through that pain.
Can you imagine a man having children?
Imagine a man being pregnant,
carrying a baby for nine months,
being sick while watching ball games.
And the birth
with the midwife saying,
"PUSH, MR JOHNSON, PUSH."

**Dogs Cannot See All Colours**
*by Mark*

If a dog could see all colours
it could drive,
stop at traffic lights,
use colour TV,
colour colouring books,
fit a plug and live to tell the tale,
give descriptions to the boys in blue,
have a favourite colour
and know what colour it was.

As well as poems based on true facts, the children might like to try inventing a few of their own. These could be quite outlandish, and you could encourage the children to tell taller and taller tales, each trying to outdo the other.

*A snail is a tortoise's favourite meal.*

*Well, my tortoise eats burgers.*

*That's nothing! Last night my tortoise went out and caught a rabbit, then skinned it and barbecued it with a sauce made from worms and rainwater.*

*That's nothing...*

*and so on.*

*And did you know that sharks are unable to surf?*

**Sharks Can't Surf**
*by Ami*

It doesn't matter how good your board is,
it doesn't matter how much you wax it,
sharks can't surf.
You can balance the board
but it would make no difference,
you'll never make a shark surf.
It would scare all the people
sitting on the beach
to see a shark riding the waves,
coming into the beach
with its razor-sharp teeth.
Sharks and surfing DO NOT MIX!

# Pick and mix

## Thirteen Ways of Looking at a Blackbird
*by Wallace Stevens*

I
Among twenty snowy mountains,
The only moving thing
Was the eye of the blackbird.

II
I was of three minds,
Like a tree
In which there are three
blackbirds.

III
The blackbird whirled in the
autumn winds.
It was a small part of the
pantomime.

IV
A man and a woman
Are one.
A man and a woman and a
blackbird
Are one.

V
I do not know which to prefer,
The beauty of inflections
Or the beauty of innuendoes,
The blackbird whistling
Or just after.

VI
Icicles filled the long window
With barbaric glass.
The shadow of the blackbird
Crossed it, to and fro.
The mood
Traced in the shadow
An indecipherable cause.

VII
O thin men of Haddam,
Why do you imagine golden
birds?
Do you not see how the
blackbird
Walks around the feet
Of the women about you?

VIII
I know noble accents
And lucid, inescapable rhythms;
But I know, too,
That the blackbird is involved
In what I know.

IX
When the blackbird flew out of
sight,
It marked the edge
Of one of many circles.

*continued...*

X
At the sight of blackbirds
Flying in a green light,
Even the bawds of euphony
Would cry out sharply.

XI
He rode over Connecticut
In a glass coach.
Once, a fear pierced him,
In that he mistook
The shadow of his equipage
For blackbirds.

XII
The river is moving.
The blackbird must be flying.

XIII
It was evening all afternoon.
It was snowing
And it was going to snow.
The blackbird sat
In the cedar-limbs.

## • Learning by example

This exercise brings together several techniques to produce a descriptive poem. Wallace's Blackbird poem is very difficult to understand. Its dense, elliptical and symbolic language can be daunting. Explain to the children that you don't expect them to have all the answers right away – but that you are going to read a poem and you'd like them to tell you what it's about.

Read the poem.

Ask for general explanation. Ask if they like the poem. Now read again the first verse and discuss it.

*Among twenty snowy mountains,*
*The only moving thing*
*Was the eye of the blackbird.*

They might suggest that it sets the scene – it paints a picture. Or that it contrasts the epic scale of the view with the tiny detail of the blackbird's eye. The scene is still – which contrasts with the movement of the eye. You might ask them if the verse rhymes or if it has a rhythm. It does have a rhythm – but not an obvious one. It does not have an obvious pattern.

Now try the same thing again, asking the children to discuss verse IX. This verse seems to be describing the blackbird through geometry.

*When the blackbird flew out of sight,*
*It marked the edge*
*Of one of many circles.*

Then try verse VII which has a Biblical or even mythic feel.

I think we can agree that it's not an easy poem. Its thirteen verses, each describing a blackbird from a different perspective, do not give up their secrets easily. Many children will enjoy the challenge of trying to decipher the poem, but many will give you blank looks and some may even feel daunted and unsure what is expected of them. For these children try to keep the discussion fun. You should ask the children if they like it. You might even ask them if they think it really *is* a poem. If someone says they think it's rubbish – then you may accept that answer – but only if it can be justified.

Now read the following poem and discuss each verse. They should find it much easier than the first one.

**Six Hoots**
*by Roger Stevens*

Oh Owl
Your eyes are two moons
Shining above the castle
In the dead of night.

Oh Owl
You are like a sonic missile
Seeking the tiny flutter
Of a heartbeat

Oh Owl
With your magical message
For the young master.

Oh Mouse
Can't you read?
Danger
Low-flying owls

Oh Owl, you scowl
When you hear
The night bell
And the wolf howl
In your cloak of darkness
That you wear so well

Oh Owl. You call me
In a nightmare, and I wake
In the frosty dawn

The first verse is pure description.
*Oh Owl*
*Your eyes are two moons*
*Shining above the castle*
*In the dead of night.*

The second verse is a simile.
*Oh Owl*
*You are like a sonic missile*
*Seeking the tiny flutter*
*Of a heartbeat*

Verse three is a literary reference
(to Harry Potter).
*Oh Owl*
*With your magical message*
*For the young master*

Verse four is a warning.
*Oh Mouse*
*Can't you read?*
*Danger*
*Low-flying owls*

Verse five is in rhyme.
*Oh Owl, you scowl*
*When you hear*
*The night bell*
*And the wolf howl...*

And finally the sixth verse is a
haiku.

For their own poem, ask the children to choose an animal. Suggest they go for something unusual – or at least not an obvious choice such as a cat or dog – there are already too many poems about cats and dogs! Their first poem will use *Six Hoots* as a model. Verse one a description, verse two a simile (or possibly a metaphor – *Oh Owl, you are like a sonic missile...*), verse three a literary reference and so on. Further drafts of the poem might use other styles or forms – a kenning or a verse written from a Biblical standpoint for example. The final draft, like the blackbird poem, should have a certain air of mystery, of making the reader do some of the work to unlock its secrets.

The verses in the following examples are written in different styles. You might like to read one or two of them to the children to see if they can identify what they are. Or ask the children to share their own poems to see if they can be decoded.

### What is a Starling?
*by Eleanor*

Millions of starry specks
Infinite chaos on the breast of
A starling

You are a gutter child, tough
and proud
Never to accept your fate

What do you call an infant star?
A star-ling – its fire
Concealed within you

Inside the streamlined wings
A delicate set of hollow
toothpicks
A fragile bone network

Perched on the window ledge
How can you stay unharmed
In that thorny hedge?

Please do not feed the starlings.
If they think you have food
Expect extreme pecking!

Chirping in outrage
Daring the world to harm you
Then fluttering off.

### Six Bites on an Arm
*by James*

The swamp is silent
Apart from the low-pitched grunt
Of the scaled and scary
Crocodile!

Like a sneaky fox
He attacks with jaws full of
Power and Grace, he is the…
Crocodile!

Tick tock, tick tock
He goes as he prepares
To pounce on hooks and hands…
Crocodile!

The crocodile is ferocious and fierce
With his extremely sharp teeth
Through your skin he will pierce
Angry, attacking and awesome
He walks slyly, on all fours

Croc is attacking
Watch out! Watch out! Watch out! Look!
He has killed someone.

*by Billy*

Whale.
Blue and Slippery.
Massive and beautiful.
The gentle giant with glinting eyes.
Whale.

You are a huge child.
Enormous
But harmless and safe.

The whale and the sparrow.
They could not be friends.
For one was deep in the ocean and the other took to the sky.
You hear the calming cry of the whale,
And the sparrow,
Who weeps in the morning.

Whale splashes his tail into the sea
And makes the tiny plankton scream and shout and flee.
The whale sings sad and lonely.
But little krill he frightens only.

The whale is large
But we should not be scared
For he is friendly.

The wonderful whale wanders Westward
Onward, outward to seek new waters.

# From the Celtic

- Of the big and the powerful

### I am Taliesin
*unknown*

I am Taliesin. I sing perfect metre
Which will last to the end of the world.
My patron is Elphin.
I know why there is an echo in a hollow;
Why silver gleams; why breath is black; why liver is bloody;
Why a cow has horns; why a woman is affectionate;
Why milk is white; why holly is green;
Why a kid is bearded; why a cow-parsnip is hollow;
Why brine is salt; why ale is bitter;
Why the linnet is green and berries red:
Why a cuckoo complains, why it sings;
I know where the cuckoos of summer are in winter.
I know what beasts there are at the bottom of the sea;
How many spears in battle; how many drops in a shower;
Why a river drowned Pharaoh's people;
Why fishes have scales,
Why a white swan has black feet...

I have been a blue salmon,
I have been a dog, a stag, a roebuck on the mountain,
A stock, a spade, an axe in the hand,
A stallion, a bull, a buck,
A grain which grew on a hill,
I was reaped and placed in an oven,
I fell to the ground when I was being roasted
And a hen swallowed me.
For nine nights I was in her crop.
I have been dead, I have been alive,
I am Taliesin

This idea for writing a poem was developed by the writer Jackie Wills, who has generously allowed us to feature it in this book. Our interpretation may be slightly different from hers.

Start the session by asking children to give themselves a new name. Not another name like Sean, David or Rebecca, but a name that means The Powerful One or All Powerful. Suggest that they could take a word that means strong, powerful, or amazing and then change it to a name. For example – Fantasticus, Magnificento, Fabuloso or Supremus.

Next ask the children this: If you could ask one question of a super, all-powerful being and know that you would be given the correct answer, what question would you ask? Warn them that they should think very carefully and not waste the opportunity with questions that science can already answer. The question should be one that could change their lives, if they knew that the answer was absolutely true. Questions like – Is there a Heaven? What happens when we die? Is God real?

Now read the poem above – *I am Taliesin*. Tell the children that it was written over 800 years ago. Ask them what questions they would ask Taliesin.

Explain to the children that they will be writing a new version of this poem. In the poem they will be boasting, like Taliesin, of the things they know and what they have been. They will be using their new name and the question that they thought of originally could be used in the poem too. You might point out that not all of Taliesin's boasts are of great and important things. Many are strange and unimportant, for example: **Why a white swan has black feet**. Who really wants to know the answer to that?

You could put the following structure on the board for the children to follow but explain that it is only there as a starting point, and that you would be happy for them to modify it or expand it to make the poem their own. The children can make a selection of lines beginning with some or all of these suggestions.

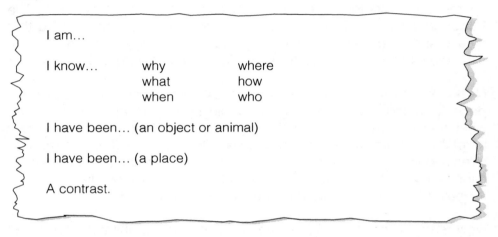

I am...

I know...      why      where
               what     how
               when    who

I have been... (an object or animal)

I have been... (a place)

A contrast.

Point out that Taliesin doesn't really say much about the objects and creatures he has been, whether in his present life or in previous lives. Rather than suggest they write a line like *I have been a wolf* – encourage the children to stretch their ideas. For example – *I have been a wolf* might become *I have been a white wolf howling in a midnight forest*.

You could suggest a new section, for instance – I have been... (a place).

*I have been hiding in the depths of an ancient forest.*

*I have circled Jupiter's moons.*

Finally ask the children to finish with a line that contains a contrast. The final line of Taliesin was 'I have been dead, I have been alive.' Get the children to suggest contrasts that might make a good last line. For example:

*I have been ice. I have been fire.*

*I have been a saint. I have been a devil.*

### I am Magnifico
*by Katie*

I am Magnifico.
I know why the dove brings peace.
I know how to escape from a black hole.
I know where the end of the world lies.
I know what is round the next corner.
I know when global warming will end.
I have seen what the future holds.
I can hold the world in the palm of my hand.
I have been to the tenth planet.
I have toasted marshmallows on the Earth's core.
I have been to the dream land.
I have been to the lost city of Atlantis.
I have been a raging wave frothing at the mouth.
I have been the monster lurking in your wardrobe.
I have been the paper you are reading from.
I have been the shimmering moon smiling at the stars.
I have travelled to Heaven and Hell and emerged unscathed.
I will not lend you any of my wisdom for...

I am Magnifico.

## Hurricano

*by Hannah*

I am Hurricano,
I know how birds sing,
I know why the hurricanes destroy,
I know where the greatest treasures are hidden,
I know where the lions hide,
I know who tells truth from lies,
I know when the gods are angry,
I know why the crows cry,
I know where the pirates sail.
I have been a swan in distress,
I have been the lion king in a pack of carnivorous lions,
I have been the trees that you cut down,
I have been the hurricane that destroyed your life.
I have been to the islands that are lost and forgotten,
I have been to the Pyramids of Egypt towering over mortals,
I have been to the deathly rocks that could slice you in half,
I have been into your mind, thinking what you think, feeling what you feel.
I decide who lives or dies,
I am Hurricano.

# The power of simplicity

• Locust tree in flower

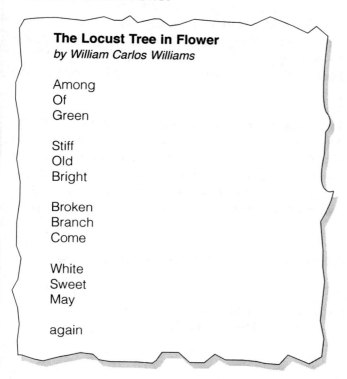

**The Locust Tree in Flower**
*by William Carlos Williams*

Among
Of
Green

Stiff
Old
Bright

Broken
Branch
Come

White
Sweet
May

again

William Carlos Williams was a master of pared-down, understated poetry written using deceptively simple language and an elegant style. This exercise is to demonstrate that a poet doesn't have to emulate the flowery and complicated language of Shakespeare's sonnets, nor does poetry have to be dense and unfathomable.

First discuss *The Locust Tree in Flower*. Ask the following questions. What does it mean? Does it look like a poem? Is it really a poem? Why did William Carlos Williams write it? Does it rhyme? Do you like it? (It's okay *not* to like a poem.)

As we have mentioned before, even with very able writers there are often a lot of blank looks, especially if they are not used to discussing poetry.

Encourage a lively debate. You are hoping that someone will notice the poem's Impressionistic quality (like Impressionist paintings that up close are a meaningless array of splodges and dots but from a distance become recognisable – similarly posters and computer images) and someone may spot that each verse could represent a season and that the poem is cyclic.

Now ask the children to write two simple sentences about an object. It can be a common, everyday object such as a table, or something more interesting, such as an antique spoon. The first sentence should describe the object simply and clearly. The second sentence should show how the writer feels about it. The sentences need to be written in a large, clear script, with a space between each word – because they are going to be cut out!

*A table is a wooden piece of furniture with a flat top and four legs. I like heavy oak tables.*

Cut the words out and arrange them randomly one below the other. Now copy out as a poem in the style of *The Locust Tree*.

*Heavy*
*Tables*
*A*
*Wooden*
*Oak*
*Like*
*Is*
*Flat*

Now repeat the exercise using a more meaningful subject, perhaps something that interests them, or moves them in some way. Kieran has written about a graveyard.

**Graveyard**
*by Kieran*

Among
The
Silent
Stiff
Secretive

Stone
Rust
Death
Whisper
Creak

Groan
Moan
Howl
Whistle
Still

Black
Cold
Emotionless
Wordless
Nothing

**September**
*by Roger Stevens*

leaf
fall
gold

wet
rake
deck

chair
conkers
rolled

beach
ball
get

burst
scars
cold

ache
first
frost

Explain that, with so few words in the poem, each word becomes very important. Tell them to consider how different combinations of words work. They are looking for ways that words may affect one another and for surprising juxtapositions. Words can be left out. New words can be added.

Words can be grouped in pairs, or in threes. Tell the children to look for rhymes – not only at the ends of lines but also verb rhymes, consonant rhymes and alliteration. In his poem *September*, Roger has tried to create a pattern of rhymes, both obvious and less so. You could read the children the poem and ask them if they can see all of the rhymes.

Your writers could look at other poems by William Carlos Williams, discuss them and take one as a model for another poem, creating it in a similar way to this.

## The power of metaphor

**Untitled**
*by Joe*

With his owl-like features this old grandfather clock
ticks away for eternity,
never missing a tick and never forgetting a tock.
Like a rocking chair he creaks with the damage of time and
suffering.
He is the autumn, the cold breath of the wind
and the many colours of the fallen leaves.
He is the putt of the golf ball as the crowd cheers a hole in one.
His robes imply the power that he holds.
He is the taste of fine wine touching your lips
and the crystal glass in your hand.
He is the empty mansion rattling with loneliness and gliding with
ideas.
He is the lone warrior,
one voice to cry through the battlefront
and bring peace at last.

**Tracy Beaker**
*by Tracey*

She is a bed that you can curl up on, on a cold, stormy night.
She is a warm but very scary tiger
She is a loud bang of thunder and lightning
She is a child of disappointment
She is a draughty and cramped mansion
She is a bright person in jeans and a tee shirt
She is a pretend writer at the moment
She will be a superb writer in the future
She is a laptop full of stories.

• What would I be?

This idea has been around for a long time, but we make no apologies for including it here as it works so well, particularly with able writers, who can easily make that leap from being literal to working with metaphor.

The idea originally appeared in Sandy Brownjohn's *Does it Have to Rhyme?*, and our version comes from *Jumpstart* by Cliff Yates.

Ask for a volunteer. The pupil stands up. You then ask the pupil to think of a well-known person, but not tell anyone who it is. The person can be a film star, a singer, a television personality, a sportsperson or a politician. The person could be a historical figure such as Henry VIII or William Shakespeare. The person could be a character from a book or a film.

Now ask the volunteer: If the person you're thinking of was an item of furniture what would he or she be? A common response to this question is one of disbelief. An item of furniture?!? You're joking! But persevere. The pupil will think of something. You might suggest that a large person might be a wardrobe, a slow, sleepy person a bed and so on. Ask for detail – what kind of wardrobe? A big old-fashioned oak wardrobe with lots of decorative bits – or a small modern wardrobe with lots of mirrors? On the board write – *Furniture* and the pupil's answer.

Now ask question two. If the person were a type of weather or a season of the year what would he or she be? Again write the question and the response on the board.

Continue asking further questions. If the person were some kind of food or drink, an item of clothing, a musical instrument, an animal, a vehicle or some kind of transport, what would he or she be?. Ask other pupils to suggest categories. (A landscape, a building, a sport...)

Finally see if anyone can guess who the person is.

Now everyone has a go. Go through the list again while each pupil writes his or her response. At the end they take turns in guessing each other's characters.

For the final poem you may choose anyone to write about. It doesn't have to be a celebrity. It could be a parent, a teacher or a friend. Explain that, although it begins with a list, each line needs to be stretched or expanded. In Joe's poem (page 84) his first line – *he is a grandfather clock* – became a grandfather clock ticking away for eternity. He then incorporated 'owl-like' into the line – imbuing it with a sense of Hogwarts, where this person works. (Can you guess who it is yet?)

Remember that every item on the list doesn't have to be used. Discuss with the children how this method of writing a poem could be adapted. It could be an opportunity, too, to talk about simile and metaphor and how they work in poetry.

## Queen Elizabeth the First

*by Charlotte*

She is a perfect blue sky,
But suddenly a swirling storm.
She is an eccentric dress, dripping with pearls.
She is a stylish, fluffy, Persian cat
Who is soft and sweet.
She is a cold winter's day on the surface,
But a warm and passionate fire inside.
She is pure-white, strong but soft.
She is peace before anger.
She is the Goddess of the Moon.

## My Grandmother

*by Bethany*

She is a clock ticking away time.
She is a library waiting for people to visit her.
She is a bright, starry night guiding my way.
She is whisky, so flavoursome and sweet.
She is spring, when things start to grow, give beautiful flowers
and fresh leaves.
She is the colour green, vibrant and natural.
She is frustration, always wanting more.
She is, and always will be, my Grandmother.

**Neil Armstrong**
*by Liam*

He is a seat waiting for his long-life dream
He is a rocket shooting up into the starry sky
He is a white spacesuit walking on the moon
He is canned tuna in a rocket out in space
He is a starry sky, loads of balls of gas
He is an alien, living in outer space, on the moon
He is moon-rock and dirt
Reflecting light from the sun.

**Energy Boy**
*by Vusani*

He is a dentist chair
moving all the time
but never still
He is Spring time,
the time for energy.
He is a cheetah
always on the move
when hunting.
And a pair of trainers
ready to run a mile.
As well as Coke
ready to explode
if shaken.

# A sense of loss

**Six Things I Lost**
*by Josie*

One was a toy grey seal that I lost somewhere on the outskirts of Cambridge.
Two was a ginger tom called George who I loved dearly.
Three was the tremendous sight of a turtle swimming in a clear blue sea.
Four was an old short-sighted grey haired lady who had many thoughts.
Five was the stone thatched cottage which was set deeply in the country.
Six were the days that slipped by year after year.

• Focus and feelings

Begin by discussing with the children how we are always losing things, and how this continues throughout our lives. Now ask them to name things that they have lost and draw up a list on the board. These things might include toys, money, clothes, teeth, watches, pets, friends and sometimes family members. Discuss with them other, less tangible, things you can lose. Fights, for example, your temper, a race or a sense of humour. You can also be filled with a sense of loss – when a holiday is over, when you move house or when a person or a pet dies.

Now ask the children to write a poem based upon a list of six things they have lost, things that were important, or are still important, to them. Encourage them to say something about each item and if they wish, instead of numbers, include the numbers in the structure of the poem, as Josie has in the opening example.

As an alternative approach to *Six Things I Lost,* ask the children to imagine they have a container (this could be a sack, a box, a jar or a chest) and that inside the container they will find everything they have ever lost.

The writer Anne Tyler in her novel **Breathing Lessons** writes about a meeting with an old man in a nursing home who believed that once he reached the Pearly Gates of Heaven, all that he had lost in his lifetime would be given back to him in a gunnysack by Saint Peter. Maggie, the main character in the book, thinks of what she might find in her sack and as well as tangible things, such as umbrellas, single earrings, 1950s skirts and a necklace, she finds the smells, sights and sounds of a summer evening, along with... a bottle of wind, a box of fresh snow.

Here are some ideas that you might suggest to the children for poems using this format. The best meal you've ever eaten, the best smell, taste, sound, view, the best thing that anyone has ever said to you, the best feeling you've ever had, the best moment of your best-ever holiday. Encourage them to write about their memories in a way that will allow a reader to share in their experiences.

**My Chest**
by Clare

In my chest I would hope to find:
The Teddy Bear my Mum gave to the jumble sale when I was at school,
The money that was stolen from my pocket when I wasn't looking,
The house points I lost when I was misbehaving,
The fish, rabbit and hamsters that died when I was a little girl,
The taste of melting marshmallows.

These ideas can be developed further through an exploration of feelings associated with loss. Discuss with the children which kind of losses would upset them the most and which they would simply shrug off. Further poems may be written which focus on the moment of loss and answer such questions as where, how, when, why, and how they felt at the time. Some children may have had experiences of bereavement and, although the notion of death shouldn't be dwelt upon, they may wish to write about what happened.

**If I Left School**
*by Charlotte*

If I left my school
I'd remember the time my friends said they'd seen a ghost
and the war for the corner of the top quad.
I'd miss being scared there'd be a burglar hiding as I
was going home
and the clay my friend said was camel poo from Africa.
I'd miss painting ink on my nails when I got bored
and the prickly hedge, and the house we live in.
I'd miss clubs we never did anything about
and everlasting lectures by the headmaster during assembly.
I'd remember the war with my friends in Class 3
and the sleepover in the cold dark gym.
If I left my school.

For another variation of this theme, ask the children if any of them have moved house or changed schools, or even lived in a different country. You might share with the children your own experiences of leaving somewhere and tell them what you miss and about your happy and sad memories.
Brian talks about leaving a house that he lived in close to the beach. When he left, he missed the fifth stair because it always creaked. He and his wife got used to jumping over the fifth stair, especially at night when the noise could wake their daughters. He missed the boxer dogs next door, the ducks who brought their new family round to see them each spring, the frogs in the ditch across the road that croaked loudly on wet nights, and the jungle, an overgrown area at the bottom of the garden. He tells the children about finding a toad living under a drain cover and the night of the 1987 hurricane when the wind whipped pebbles up from the beach and smashed all the front windows of the house, blew off the garage roof and blew down its walls and blew down two trees from the jungle onto the remains of the garage.

Now ask the children what they think they would miss if they were to move house. Emphasise that it is the little details that are important.

Explain that the phrases 'my big bedroom' or 'my huge garden' would make dull lines in this type of poem as lots of people have these – but rather try to find something special to say. For example, a hiding place, a quick route through the hedge to next door, a creaky floorboard, a strange mark on the wall, noises from the radiators at night, a tree house or the smell of wild garlic.

Next ask the children to think of what they would miss and what they might later remember if they left their house or somewhere meaningful to them, such as their village or their country. Remind them to look for details. If the poem is going to be about a school – think about the quiet places where they might like to curl up and read, the spooky art room cupboard or teacher's desk piled high with all sorts of junk.

Their poem could be written from their own point of view, or from the point of view of someone else. What do they think their mum would miss about their house? Or what would their cat or dog miss? What places are important to a dog or cat?

Bear in mind that it is the tiny details that will make this piece come to life. In Charlotte's poem, above, she avoids ordinary lines such as 'I'd miss all the teachers and my friends' and finds some great images and personal details such as the clay that was like camel's poo and painting her fingernails with ink.

## Shorts

• *Good and bad*

This is a simple idea that can be extended in all sorts of ways. First ask the children to make a list of good things and bad things. For example – things they like or dislike about school or their good habits and bad habits. Alternatively compare their bad habits with a friend's good habits, or why their mum is good and they are bad. Instead of good and bad other opposites could be used such as happy and sad, calm and anxious and so on.

It begins as a list of maybe ten things and then can be extended rhythmically or with rhyme, or into any of a number of poetic styles such as rap, rhyming couplets, personal explorations or nonsense.

### Why I'm Bad and My Best Mate's Good
*by Daisy*

I am bad because I fall out easily
My best mate's good because she makes friends
I'm bad because I'm a slob
My best mate's good because she keeps fit.
I'm bad because I get moody very easily.
My best mate's good because she stays calm
I'm bad because I don't care what I look like
My best mate's good because she does.

### Like or Hate?
*by James*

I like science
But I hate school
I like to recycle
I hate to throw away
I like to share
I hate to be greedy
There are so many things I like and hate
I can't list them all

• That's nonsense!

### The Trouble With Geraniums
*by Mervyn Peake*

The trouble with geraniums
Is that they're much too red
The trouble with my toast is that
It's far too full of bread

The trouble with a diamond
Is that it's much too bright
The same applies to fish and stars
And the electric light

The trouble with the stars I see
Lies in the way they fly
The trouble with myself is all
Self-centred in the eye

The trouble with my looking-glass
Is that it shows me, me;
There's trouble in all sorts of things
Where it should never be.

Generally speaking, children have challenges with rhyming – not so much with finding rhymes but with understanding how to choose an appropriate rhyme. This is a very straightforward and quick way to produce a fun, rhyming poem.

Make three columns on the board. In the first ask the children to suggest words meaning good, for the beginnings of each line. For example, *What's great about, pleasing, wonderful, fantastic*… and so on. In the middle column write some names of animals beginning with the same sounds as the words in the first column. So we may have *What's pleasing about penguins* or *What's intriguing about iguanas*.

The third column is for the ends of the lines. But explain that they are going to write lines three and four first – before they write the first two lines. Explain that this is a common 'trick' that poets use. It's much better to disguise a weak rhyme by placing it at the beginning or in the middle of a verse.

The third and fourth rhymes might thus be –

What's pleasing about penguins
Is their little waiters' suits

or

What's intriguing about iguanas
Is the way they flick their tongues.

Now ask them to write the first and second lines. To do this, in the first example, they need a rhyme for suit – and in the second a rhyme for tongues.

### What's Magnificent About a Monkey
*by Lucy*

What's magnificent about a monkey is
How it swings from different trees
What's happy about a hamster is
Its cute and tiny knees

What's cracking about a cat is
It's gorgeous and it's furry
What's brill about a bull is
The way it deals with fury

What's excellent about an elephant is
Its big and flappy ears
What's cool about a camel is
It's been around for years

Their final poem need not be about animals, of course, but should have a unifying theme as in this verse.

**Untitled**
*by Cydni*

The perfection of paper clips is
The way they clip to paper
The surprising thing about staples is
The way they fit a stapler

Similarly the poem could be about scary things (start with a list of other words for scary) or weird, or some other emotion. What's scary about spiders, what's really weird about spider's webs and so on.

Equally important in this poem is the rhythm. Encourage the children to read their first draft out loud and to find words and combinations of words that fit the *di dum di dum di dum* beat. They could use a different beat – then the important thing would be to keep each verse the same.

di dum di dum di dum
di dum di dum di

• The Sound of Music

**My Not Favourite Things**
*by Roger Stevens*

Doorknobs and chickens
And Rice Dream and chocolates
Sunshine and moonshine
And ice cream in pockets
Spent tunes and bent spoons
Bananas with wings
These are a few of my not favourite things

Kiwis with spots on
And rides in the evenings
TV with lots on
And Spiderman key rings
Thistles and whistles
And some songs of Sting's
These are a few of my less favourite things

When the pear drops
When a bear plops
When I grow a beard
I simply revarnish my old bits of string
And then I don't feeeeeeeeeeeeeeeeeeeeeeellll
Soooooooooooooo
Weird

With this exercise, do as we do and simply read the children the poem and let them figure it out for themselves. It's ideal if you have a spare ten minutes to fill. You might present it as a challenge. The children have to fit both the rhyme and the rhythm to make it work. When they've finished they could sing it to the class.

This idea came from Eton End School that Roger was visiting and where a group of pupils sang to him their version of his poem.

We should also add that since putting together this piece for this book we have found a version of *My Favourite Things* by Carol Ann Duffy, which you might like to search out. So – how about a new version of – How Do You Solve a Problem with a Teacher?

**Not Favourite Things**
*by Joe*

Cold chicken pieces
And Rhianna singles
Fresh onion salad
And radio jingles
Drain pipes and fresh tripe
And chocolate rings
These are a few of my not favourite things.

**The Scariest Things**
*by Chloe*

Creaks in the attic
And bats in the moonlight
Witches on broom sticks
And Halloween at night
Devils that cackle
And snake bite that stings
These are a few of my scariest things

• Beginning, middle and end

**First Day at a New School**
by Jamie

A feeling in the stomach
like rats crawling around
Looking at the clock
as the hands move much too fast
Mum calls out, Time to go.
Sitting in the classroom
laughing at the teacher's corny jokes
Making a new friend
who also supports Chelsea
Eating in the strange canteen
that sounds like an aircraft hangar
Mum says, What did you do today?
You know, I say,
Just this and that.
And how was it, she says?
You know, I say,
okay.

Teachers spend a lot of time telling their students that stories have to have a beginning, a middle and end. By which, of course they mean a story should start well and win the reader over, that it should have a satisfying conclusion and that the middle of the story should develop the story's plot.

Ask the children to think of either an event from their own lives or a relationship they have had with someone. The event or relationship must be real and it should be an event or relationship that has now ended.

It could be a day at school – maybe the first day in a new form – or a holiday, the school play, a football match that the pupil played in or watched (but in real life – not on the television). It could be a friend whom the pupil no longer sees, a family member or a pet that has died. (This exercise can produce some quite personal and powerful pieces of work.)

Now ask the children to think about the beginning of that event or relationship. What happened leading up to it? How did it begin? How did the pupil feel about it?

Give the children a few minutes to write down all that they can about the beginning of the event/relationship. Stress that they are just putting their ideas down on paper at this time and that they are not yet writing a poem or a story. You are simply looking for information that can be used in the later piece.

Repeat this exercise with the middle of the event/relationship and then with its ending.

This exercise could be used to write prose or a poem. Write about another event – but if the earlier one was in prose write this as a poem or vice versa.

Discuss the idea of the beginning, middle and end, with reference to books the children have read.

# Serious issues

Able writers should be given the opportunity to write about more serious concerns. Writing, as we know, can be very therapeutic. The act of writing can help us, and the children in our charge, come to terms with things that may have never been properly addressed. We are not advocating a form of psychotherapy here – rather commenting on the fact that writing can be a useful tool for a teacher in a classroom situation.

More importantly from the point of view of this book, writing about more serious and personal issues can produce both revealing and illuminating, and often quite powerful, poetry and prose.

Writing of this kind will usually need considerable input and discussion prior to anything being put on paper. This isn't the flippant confession, but a chance to discuss with the children real issues that affect them.

A good topic to begin with is bullying. A discussion about this, if any of the children have been victims of bullies, or have witnessed it, can produce some very sensitive pieces of work.

### Shame or Fame?
*by Alice*

How would you feel
If someone came up to you in the playground
And picked on you, like a flock of angry vultures,
pecking at your blistered skin?

Here they come again!
The monsters that haunt my stories,
The angry vultures that peck at my feelings,
The colossal giants that take away the thought –
Of a whispering wish.

The winged tormentors that drop down on you,
The squabbling curses that poison your life forever.
The deep dark hole that will darken your life...
Tell – Release the Curse

• Share a dare

A session on dares can also be revealing. Children understand what it is like to be dared to do something and how unpleasant it can be for them if they refuse. As a child Brian remembers being dared to climb a cliff to reach a cave. Looking back, he says, scares him even now – but he survived. He says he must have been holding the hands of angels! Perhaps you have a similar experience of a dare that you could share with the children?

**Dared**
*by Ann*

They all remember
The day they dared
Sarah-Ann,
She was really scared.
They laughed and jeered
And coaxed her on,
But when she fell
The smiles were gone.
She began to scream,
They began to run,
The younger kids cried,
The fear had begun.
Somebody fainted,
Somebody laughed,
But the way it came out
Was hysterical and hard.
Then they heard it,
The sirens were coming.
The police and the ambulance
rushing towards them.
But as they arrived
Her screaming was silenced.
Sarah-Ann died
When she fell from the pylons.

# Getting Ahead:
# Mainly Prose

# Creating a character

This is probably the most important component of a story. People read stories because they care about the central characters. They want to know what will happen to the character next: What will he or she do? How will it all turn out? A reader will often struggle to the end of a bad novel if they care about the character. But if the character isn't 'real', then a reader will give up, even if the writing is good. Characters also drive the plot along.

Even able writers can find delineating a character difficult. They tend to step out of character, or forget that their character might develop as a result of what happens. The following exercise may seem superficial – but it's a sure-fire way to create a character from nothing.

● Am I realistic?

This material also works well with less-able children. With a regular class it might be given out as a photocopied sheet or it can be done as an exercise where the teacher reads out each category and the children write their responses on paper or in their books.

Explain to the children that they are going to create a character for a story. The character should be roughly their own age and live nearby.

Then ask a series of questions such as – *Is your character a boy or a girl? How old is your character?* The answer should be written quickly, without too much thought. You are looking for a framework to hang the character on and so, at this stage, you don't want the children to agonise or take ages over this. A quick answer will give as good a result as a long, drawn-out one. Ask for the character's name last of all – the name can then match the character. Ask one or two children to read out the details of their character. It's amazing how quickly these generated characters seem to become real.

*Billy is twelve. He has brown hair. He lives in Birmingham with his mum and step-dad who works in a top-secret science laboratory. Best friend is Sid. Home life is chaotic and he spends his time outside flying model planes. He is terrified of spiders, is a good friend but is wary of authority.*

**Here are the questions to ask:**
**Gender / Date of birth / Age**
**Place of birth:**
>    Your town?
>    Your country?
>    Abroad?
>    Another planet? / Another time?

**Size:**
>    Big?
>    Fat?
>    Small?
>    Thin?

**Hair / Eyes / Unusual facial or bodily features / Mode of dress:**
>    Casual, smart, trendy, Oxfam…

**Favourite clothes / Hobbies**
**Family:**
>    Parents, brothers, sisters etc.

**Pets / Home life:**
>    Chaotic, calm, messy…

**Feelings about school / After-school clubs / Hobbies/**
**Best friends**
**Inner strength / Weakness:** These two should be internal – for example,
>    loyal, brave – rather than 'good at Football!'

**Fears**
**Name:** It must NOT be a name of someone you know.

The character is now ready to use in a story. You might ask your children to write a short description of the character. We often ask able writers for a description in *exactly* 100 words. This focuses them on having to consider all the words they have used very carefully. Ask them if there are any unnecessary words in their descriptions – or boring facts about their characters which tell us little. The fact that Billy is scared of spiders is more interesting than the fact that his hair is brown. We then ask for another rewrite in exactly sixty words.

*Able Writers in Your School*

Discuss with the children the idea of giving their character a weakness. This is a useful device in a story. It's no accident that Indiana Jones had a fear of snakes. If they were writing a story about climbing mountains, a character with a fear of heights could make a very interesting hero.

In the sections that follow there will be several opportunities to use the characters created here. You might like to suggest that the children create several characters for future use. They could come from a range of backgrounds, be boys and girls, men and women. They might also like to create some over-the-top characters. Explain that these could have interesting 'walk-on' parts in future stories.

# Creating a setting

* The hills are alive

Sam was enjoying the sensation of the cool water on his bare feet. He was glad that the beach was deserted. He was in no mood to talk to anyone. He was thinking about the things his Mum had said. It wasn't fair that he should have to look after his sister while his mum was off enjoying herself with her boyfriend. Sam wasn't really paying attention to his surroundings which was a shame, as the sun was glittering on the water and the sky, between the clouds, was so bright and blue it made your eyes ache. Sam didn't see the piece of driftwood sticking out of the sand. He stubbed his toe, cried in pain, and fell over, right into a puddle of warm seawater.

Sam pulled himself up and carried on along the beach. He shouldn't have shouted at his sister, though, and he shouldn't have left her on her own. He was still feeling angry because she broke his Gameboy. He bent down and grabbed a large, white pebble to throw into the sea. He didn't see the wasp, using the pebble as a place to sunbathe. "Yeow!" he cried, and dropped the pebble, right on his foot.

A big cloud crossed the sun and it became suddenly dark…

Many people read books because they identify in some way with the setting – whether it be a fantasy place as in Harry Potter, or an ordinary school like their own. Would-be travellers like to read about exotic locations and would-be space explorers about other planets.

The setting, where a story takes place, can be more than simply a convenient location. It can add to the atmosphere of a story and even be an active part of the story. Again – Hogwarts comes to mind here. The behaviour of the school itself (the stairs, the pictures, the ghosts, the willow tree) can all influence the story directly.

When you write a story it is always a good idea to base it somewhere that you are familiar with. It's quite difficult, especially for children, to write about another country, for example, if they've never been there. In this exercise we ask the children to make the setting more than just a convenient location for a story's plot.

Discuss with the children places where they've been on holiday.

Then ask them to imagine what it would be like if their holiday place became antagonistic, deliberately aggressive, towards them. Ask them: *What if the sand on the beach made a point of getting in your shoes and the sea was determined to throw up lots of dangerous jellyfish? What if the castle you were exploring seemed to be deliberately dropping lumps of rock aimed at your head?*

Tell them they are going to write an account of going for a walk on holiday. At first all is well and they are enjoying exploring a new place. But gradually things begin to happen that make the walk less enjoyable. For example, they step in a hole and lose their balance, twist an ankle, get stung by nettles and then get very wet in a downpour. Things go from bad to worse and they start to believe that the place itself is out to get them. They begin to panic!

After the first drafts have been shared and discussed, explain that the bad things that happen need to be well spaced out. Maybe matching the pace of the story. If the character is walking have several sentences between each event. The sentences could be quite long. They could be descriptive, or we could learn the character's thoughts. If the character is running, the events could come more quickly, the sentences shorter. As the momentum builds so the gaps between events shorten, each one happening a little sooner to build up momentum.

Remind the children that the first draft is really to produce something to work on and improve. Writers make these sorts of decisions all the time. Should a sentence be long or short? Does the story have a fast pace or a slow pace? Or a quickening pace?

The story needs an introduction. Rather than just describing the character and the scene, let the reader learn about the scene and the character through things that happen – the action – or through the character's dialogue or speech. Read them the example above and discuss this.

Discuss with the children how a story like this might end. In the example above there are two stories. The first is the actual physical story – the beach seemingly attacking Sam. The second is taking place in Sam's head. He's left his sister on her own.

# Plot

Narrative is the process of telling a story. It's a journey. Plot refers to its structure. It's a map. Here is a simple exercise that looks at one way of plotting a story.

Many stories take other stories as their starting point. A good example is *Romeo and Juliet*. In 1530 Luigi Da Porto published *A Story Newly Found of Two Noble Lovers*. In 1554 Matteo Bandello wrote a novella called *Giulietta e Romeo*. In 1580 William Painter wrote a story based on this and earlier in 1562 Arthur Brooke wrote a poem called *The Tragicall Historye of Romeus and Iuliet*. Scholars are pretty much in agreement that Shakespeare will have read all four of these sources for his play. Since Shakespeare there have been many versions of this story based on his play. An opera, a ballet, a musical (West Side Story), a comedy (Romanoff and Juliet), a punk version (Tromeo and Juliet) and many, many more.

## • Cinderella plus

Take a well-known fairy story or pantomime for the basis of a story. For example – Cinderella.
Discuss with the children – and write down in simple list form – the key points of the plot. The list might look something like this.

- Ugly sisters get invited to ball.
- They taunt Cinderella.
- She whinges to Buttons.
- Sisters go to the Ball.
- Cinders is all alone and fed up.
- Fairy Godmother arrives.
- Changes objects to ball gown, coach etc.
- Warning: back by midnight – or else!
- Cinderella dances with Prince at the Ball.
- Clock chimes.
- Cinderella drops slipper.
- Prince searches land for Cinderella.
- He finds her.

Discuss how this could be used as the plot for a new story.
For example, it could be set in modern times. Instead of a ball it's a disco.
Or a party. Instead of a prince – a film star.

Or it could be given a different setting. What if the characters were all animals? You could have a very different story simply by changing Cinderella's character. What if, instead of a whiny victim, she was a get-up-and-go, feisty heroine? Would Lara Croft have sat at home and complained? Or Catwoman? Or what if Cinderella wasn't interested in wealth and the trappings of celebrity and fashion? Or if she were a he?

Brainstorm this and see how many different ideas, as wild and far-out as possible, your writers can come up with. They could each write their own version of Cinderella, or could try their hand using a different source.

Before writing the story discuss its tone. Will it be serious, silly, funny, moving or scary?

Talk about its protagonist. Remind them that the central character should be sympathetic. It's always a good idea for readers to identify with the main character in a story.

Finally, discuss how the story might end.

Now – write out an outline, based on the one above. And write the story.

As an alternative exercise, you could get hold of a copy of Roald Dahl's *Revolting Rhymes*. (Your school will probably already have one.) Ask the children to write a poem using this technique.

# Dialogue

"Which Floor?"

'Four, please,' Andrew said.

The lift doors closed. The lift began to rise. The two boys stared at the floor, neither wanting to speak.

Andrew watched the lights gradually move. From ground floor to floor one. From one to two. He wondered where the other boy was getting out. From two to three. From three to...

There was a shudder. The lift lurched and stopped. Andrew looked at the boy. The boy looked back.

'What happened?' Andrew said.

'The lift's stuck.'

'It will probably start up again in a minute.'

'Of course it will,' Andrew said. But Andrew felt worried. He remembered his uncle telling him how he'd once been stuck in a lift for three hours. 'Yes, any minute now.'

- Trapped in a lift

Dialogue is one of the most important elements of a story. As in real life, characters use it to communicate with one another in a story. It is also used to communicate with us, the readers. Good dialogue will keep us involved and interested. Chances are that if you're ever tempted to skip a section of prose in a book you're reading it won't be the dialogue.

*Dialogue is denoted by quotation marks. In the UK we tend to use 'single' marks. As a general rule quotation marks go outside punctuation marks. If you're unsure do it this way and you'll probably be right. Start a new paragraph when changing speakers. (A good book on grammar will give you the full story.)*

Able writers should be happy to write several drafts of a piece of work. This exercise takes the idea of rewriting a piece several times, each time adding to it and changing it until the desired goal is reached. Ask the children if they've ever been in a lift and to describe the circumstances. Was it on holiday, in a hotel? Or was it in a big department store? What did the lift look like – both outside and inside? What did the sensation of travelling in a lift feel like?

Now ask them to write an account, around 100 words, about two children trapped in a lift. They do not know one another. Keep the story very simple. The idea is to write an outline that can be fleshed out into a proper story. Use as much dialogue as you can, keeping description or narrative to an absolute minimum.

Ask two or three of the children to share their outlines. Now explain that, to make the story more interesting, each character will have a back story. This is the story of the character before he (or she) got into the lift. For example, perhaps the characters met the day before and fell out. Perhaps they argued about whose turn it was to ride on the roller coaster, or maybe one accidentally knocked the other's sand castle over. Perhaps Andrew, in the example above, gets into the lift in a really bad mood. Maybe he's claustrophobic and can only stay in the lift for a short time. Maybe he's really hungry and on his way to lunch. Discuss this with the children and ask them to decide on a back story that will make their two characters' encounter more interesting. Then ask them to write this second version of the story.

*Characters can be identified by the way they speak. Perhaps a character will have a fondness for certain words or phrases, or will always use short sentences, be prone to rambling or pontificating.*

Discuss with the children the different ways that people speak. Can they think of any examples? Characters in *Coronation Street* and in *EastEnders*, Yoda in *Star Wars*, maybe even teachers in the school! Ask them to consider the dialogue they have given their two characters and add one or two touches that might help differentiate between the way that they each speak and the words they use.

*Dialogue should move the story on. When a character talks to another character it should be to convey information, either about the plot or the character.*

At this point you could ask for their final version of the lift episode. But for able writers you could push this idea further. Discuss with them the idea that there is something that we, the readers, don't know. Suggest they give one of their characters a secret that he must keep from the other character. Maybe he is in love with the other person's sister or brother. Maybe he is desperate for the loo. Challenge them to think of a way to show this through the dialogue – without actually spelling it out. Write a new version of the story.

Explain to the children that, when they are writing dialogue, the reader needs to be clear who is speaking and that the best way of conveying this is with 'he said', or 'she said'. Sometimes when only two characters are speaking you can leave this out altogether or make it obvious who is speaking by having the character do something. For example, *Jake looked at his watch. "It's three o'clock."*

Tell them that occasionally it's all right to use words such as whispered or shrieked but too many adverbs can gum up the works as in – he said *forcibly*, she averred *morosely*, he murmured *miserably*. Explain that rather than *telling* us someone is miserable it's better to *show* they are miserable through their actions. Or by what they say. As with adjectives, use adverbs sparingly.

When they have finished, ask the children to check through their stories. Are quotation marks in the right place? Does each new person's dialogue start with a new paragraph? Is it clear who is speaking? Are there too many adverbs? Could they cut any 'he saids' and 'she saids'?

Discuss their endings. Explain that readers deserve a good ending. It doesn't have to be *happy ever after,* but it should leave the reader satisfied. Having the lift suddenly plunge to the ground and kill its inhabitants is not a good idea. And neither is the lift starting up again without anything having happened. Perhaps someone could come up with a good twist.

Now completely rewrite the story – bearing all the above changes in mind.

There are many variants on this idea. The story could be written in the first person. It could feature three people trapped. The characters could be a boy and girl. This story could be longer – maybe 300–400 words. Could the children use the dialogue to introduce an element of suspense? (See Suspense, page 124.) *Any moment the lift might fall.* Instead of writing it from the point of view of dialogue – set it in one of the character's heads – as thoughts. Make it a fantasy where the characters are wizards or animals. Or Science Fiction. Or rewrite the above story as a play. In a play nearly all the information about the story and characters has to be relayed *only* through the dialogue. Maybe once it's written the children could act it out.

# Descriptive writing

• You need hands

> Dom walked into the classroom to wait for his new teacher. The rest of the class were still in the playground. It was bigger than his old classroom and untidy and Dom wondered what his new classmates would be like.
>
> "You're tall," a voice said. There was someone sitting at the back of the gloomy classroom. He looked around for the light switch.
>
> "You don't say much." The boy was scruffy-looking with long, dark hair. He kept wiping his nose with the back of his hand. "You play football?" the boy asked.
>
> "Maybe I do," Dom said. He sat in the teacher's chair, hoping his height would look less obvious. The teacher's desk was a mess. Dom picked up three pencils and two pens and put them in a neat row.
>
> The boy sniffed and poked his finger in his ear. "We need a new striker." The boy studied his finger. "And you're tall…"

When a character first appears in a story it is often useful to focus on some descriptive element of the character to help establish him or her quickly in the reader's mind. It could be the way the character dresses. It could be a nervous habit that the character has – always wringing her hands or speaking with a stutter when she's stressed. It could be a physical characteristic such as Harry Potter's scar.

For this exercise the children each need a character. Try creating one using the Creating a Character technique. (See page 105.) Ask the children to take one of their character's negative attributes – such as fear, nervousness around the opposite sex, conceit or short temper. Now ask them to think about that character's hands and what they might look like. Ask them how the character might use his or her hands in the light of the character's weakness.

Explain how an arrogant character might make a fist, or bang his hands on the table. Someone with something to hide might be forever covering parts of her face, particularly her mouth when she's speaking. Discuss this idea.

Now the children should write a brief description (one or two sentences) of the character at the beginning of a story. He or she enters a room. Briefly describe the room. There is someone else in the room. Briefly describe the other character. A dialogue develops. Use one of the character's hands to illuminate the scene. You might read out the example above and discuss what sort of characters the children might be.

Ask the children to share their descriptions. Discuss how they could be developed into stories. How could an element of conflict or drama be introduced? In the extract above maybe the two boys support rival Premiership teams. Maybe the story could end with them both in the school team, united against a common foe.

### • A room with a view

Ask the children to describe a room in their house in just fifty words. If they describe their bedroom, for example, ask them to pick out a few small details that may reveal a lot about themselves. The old Coke cans pushed under the bed with last year's clothes, the massive poster of Buffy and the giant cuddly rabbit… small details such as these can reveal a lot about a person.

The idea is to show rather than tell. Although it's okay to tell someone what a character is like in a story – that can lead to dull and uninteresting writing. Explain that it is much better to show what a character is like through his or her actions, or dialogue. This makes the character more real – and more memorable.

Showing that Nadim is an untidy person by having him perched on a pile of old clothes and playing his Gameboy which is balanced on a broken crate that once held oranges gives us a much better picture of Nadim than simply telling us that he's untidy.

Now ask the children to describe a room in a character's house in 100 words. The character may be someone they have invented (see page 105) or someone from an earlier story. Or the character could be a real person, such as a friend or member of the family. The idea is to tell us as much as possible about that character from what is in the room.

So if their character were an old lady, maybe a grandmother, what sort of room would it be? How would it be decorated? Would the walls be painted or would there be wallpaper? What would the wallpaper look like? Would the room have a carpet? What kind of furniture would there be? Would the room be very tidy or messy? Would there be photos on the walls, or pictures, or would the room be bare? These are questions the children might consider.

Small details can make the writing come alive: 'A faded photo in a tarnished silver frame of a young girl smiling at someone behind the camera.'

* Who sleeps in a room like this?

This works much the same as the two exercises above – but this time we are going to use a well-known character from fiction.

Begin by asking the children to choose a well-known fictional character and then to make a list of everything that would be found in that character's bedroom. Explain, for example, that in Dracula's bedroom the walls might be painted red and black. The room, below the castle, would have stone walls and floor. A bookcase would be carved from bone and there would be books, very specific to Dracula, on its shelves.

Organise the items on this list into some sort of order, set it into lines and then flesh it out with details. The trick is to convey who the character is without actually mentioning his or her name.

*Red and black walls, sunset and blood*
*Cobwebs in the corners*
*Crimson curtains, heavy with disappointment*
*Stone floor, hard and cold*
*Bookcase of carved bone*
*Books,* The A to B of Blood Groups
*The Life of a Bloodsucker....*

The final poem, **Who Sleeps in a Room Like This?**, could be kept as a puzzle – in which case they might want to put the most obvious 'clues' last and the most baffling at the beginning. Alternatively the character could be mentioned in the title or at the end.

This poem doesn't have to rhyme, but explain that its shape and rhythm should reflect its subject matter. In the Dracula excerpt there is a slow, measured rhythm and lots of alliteration. A poem about Winnie the Pooh, for example, would be lighter and more conversational. In that poem, rhyme would be more appropriate, as in the Winnie the Pooh stories.

# Conflict

> **Sarah**: What are you doing here?
> **Ellie**: What's it to you?
> **Sarah**: Just asking that's all.
> *There is silence for a couple of minutes.*
> **Ellie**: Anyway – it wasn't my fault.
> **Sarah**: What wasn't?
> **Ellie**: You know very well…

The basis of nearly all drama is conflict and this can make for a lively discussion about how writing is served by conflict and what, in terms of writing, the word means. Ask the children to imagine a series of *Eastenders* where everyone gets along famously and no one ever falls out with anyone else. Imagine Shakespeare's Richard III as a kindly person who only wanted to be a loyal subject and family member. That would be a very different, and boring, play.

Similarly discuss stories in which there is conflict. Does everyone at Hogwarts get along as one big jolly family? There are several conflicts going on in that story as well as the main good versus evil one. Can the children identify them? There's Harry and Malfoy, Harry and his aunt and uncle, even Harry and Ron fall out at one point. Ask the children to talk about their favourite books – or about books you've read in class – looking for the drama, looking for the conflict. Keep the discussion lively and fun.

• Is there trouble brewing?

For this, the children work in pairs and each will need a character that they have developed (see page 105) and who is waiting for a story. The characters should be around their own age and at the same school.

Be sure the children understand what conflict means in this context. It doesn't only mean fighting. It means that one character wants one thing and the other character wants something else. Both may be acceptable things to want, but they aren't compatible. Or one character may not want the other character to have what he or she wants. Conflict creates the drama and tension in a story.

The two characters are waiting outside the Head Teacher's office. They have been fighting and they know they are about to get into trouble.

The paired children should then discuss with each other what their characters might have done. Then either:
a) act out the scene (in a class or group you might ask one couple to do this first – and afterwards discuss with everyone how successful this was) or
b) write down the dialogue that the two characters use, each person taking a turn to write his or her character's speech. It can be written like a play.

Ask the children to write a short story in which two characters meet. These characters could have a 'past'. Maybe their families don't get on. Maybe one suspects the other of telling tales. Maybe they are both up for selection in the school football team – but there's only one place. Discuss other possible scenarios with the class before you begin.

Each story should include some information about the characters and plenty of dialogue. It should be written in the third person.

As an adult there will have been times in your life when you have been in arguments – and thought you were in the right. Tell the children about such an argument – and about how aggrieved you felt. Now encourage the children to share their own experiences of arguing against the odds. Ask them to write a short story in which two characters meet. They don't get on. Write it in the first person. The person telling the story believes that he or she is in the right and doesn't understand the other person's point of view. Ask what would happen if a third person appeared and took the other person's side. How would the narrator feel?

# Point of view

### • From short journeys

This exercise uses the same technique used in Dialogue, page 112, in which we ask the children to write a piece and then rewrite it several times, each time changing it and adding to it, to reach a desired outcome.

First ask the children to write an account of a short journey. It could be from home to the shops (or vice versa), from home to school, a visit to Gran's or to the park. It should be a journey that the children are familiar with. It should be written in the first person. And it should simply record things that can be seen, smelled or heard on that journey. It should be no longer than 100 words.

*I left home at half-past eight, said goodbye to Mum, closed the back door and walked up the garden path. The rooks were making a racket in the trees as always and old Mrs Smith next door had her kitchen window open and Radio 2 blaring out. I walked up the road to the bus stop. Sara was already there. We waited seven minutes for the bus...*

Now ask them to imagine that the person giving the account is expecting something bad to happen at the journey's end. Maybe she knows she will be in trouble with the Head for something she did yesterday. Or perhaps, when he gets to the park, he knows he'll have to tell his best mate that he didn't choose him for the football team. Or maybe the journey goes past the regular hang-out of the school bully.

Next they must add into the first account details that might assume an importance in the light of what will happen. They can also add the narrator's thoughts.

*I left home at half-past eight. I left it as long as I could but I didn't want to be late for school and have that added to all my other troubles. I walked slowly up the garden path, turned, and took a long, lingering look at the house, the grimy brickwork, the window of my room, the back door. Maybe it would be my last...*

Finally the children must take the first account and change it into the third person. They should give the person a name – not the name of the writer. Here we are fictionalising the name.

They can also use a literary device called *foreshadowing*. This means that narrative draws attention to something that will happen in the future, something that the writer is telling the reader, but that the protagonist doesn't know. Tell the children that now there is something nasty awaiting the person who is setting out on the journey – but he is blissfully unaware of it. However – they can give clues to the reader that something is going to happen. It's a bit like the music you get in scary films, the rumbling low notes of the cello that tell you all is not well.

*Jenny left home at half-past eight. She said goodbye to Mum with her usual big grin. She closed the back door and walked up the garden path singing softly to herself. The rooks were making a racket in the trees as always. One black rook swooped low over Jenny's head. Jenny saw the rook's shadow first and ducked. Daft bird, she said to herself and smiled. Old Mrs Smith next door had her kitchen window open and Radio 2 was blaring out. As she walked up the road to the bus stop she could hear the news blaring out. More trouble in the war against terror. Sara was usually there waiting, but not this morning. Jenny looked up. The sky was clouding over and it looked like rain.*

Then children might like to share their work with each other. Discuss with them the pros and cons of writing in the first or the third person. Which way do they prefer to work? Remind them that in the first person the reader can only ever know the things the character telling the story knows. When they come to write other stories suggest they consider whether or not to write the story in the first or third person.

# Suspense

Able writers, especially those confident with prose, tend to write very quickly, piling events up one upon another, as they get caught up in the excitement of writing. This is good, as it builds confidence in getting ideas quickly onto paper. But sometimes we need to slow things down. This exercise asks the writer to look at his or her work objectively and deliberately slow its pace to create a sense of suspense.

Explain to the children that a suspense story is the very opposite of an adventure story. In an adventure story events might happen quickly, one after another. The gap between them shortens as the pace quickens and the climax builds.

In a suspense story we know that something is going to happen but we don't know when. We are trapped in a maze. We think that the monster is around the *next* corner. But no – it's not. Then it's around the *next* corner. But no! And we try to prolong and build this anticipation as long as possible. In fact we slow the action right down.

## • Fantastical phobias

This activity was developed with children at Selston Bagthorpe Primary School in Nottinghamshire. Ask the children to think of something that scares them. Get them to choose real-life, but not too extreme, phobias – such as fear of heights, fear of spiders, of speaking in public, of getting lost on a busy beach and so on. (But be wary of turning up a real-life experience that a child had actually had that might provoke some sort of traumatic reaction. Hopefully you will know your children and just how far you can take this story.) Discuss these everyday phobias and how they affect people, or have affected them.

Now ask them to write a brief outline based around such a situation. Something like this:

1. Setting. A house.
2. Characters. Sarah and her mum.
3. Sarah is scared of dogs.
4. Mum arrives with a dog that she's looking after for a friend.
5. Mum is called away but she locks dog safely in a room.
6. Sarah hears a noise.
7. She goes to check the room is still locked but the dog has escaped.
8. She makes her way back to her bedroom.
9. She is convinced the dog will leap out and attack her any moment.
10. A satisfactory ending.

Now ask the writers to consider each stage of the outline.

1. – 4. We need to know that it's a big house – so, when the dog escapes, it has room to hide. We also need to know about Sarah's phobia. But rather than simply state it, introduce it either through the action of the story or through dialogue. (Remember *show* not *tell!*)

*"Oh good," Sarah thought. "Mum's home." As she made her way along the gloomy passageway from her room and down the narrow stairs of the big, old house, she could hear her mum closing the front door and taking off her raincoat in the hall.*

*"Hello Mum," Sarah said. "I'm glad you're…" She stopped. And shrieked. "Oh no! Mum! No!"*

*On a lead, in Mum's hand, was a dog, a border collie.*

*"This is Milo," Mum said.*

*Milo looked up at Sarah and gave a little bark, showing his sharp teeth.*

*"You know I hate dogs," Sarah said.*

5. – 9. In a suspense story it's important to set it up so that the reader knows something is going to happen. This could be a good thing – waiting for a letter to arrive with exam results, or waiting for a friend to arrive at the station. In this case though, it's bad. So the reader needs to be in no doubt that Sarah is scared of dogs.

Once the dog has escaped it is very important to string the reader along. The story can be slowed right down. Any moment the dog might appear and the writer must stress how scared Sarah is. Again try to communicate her fear through her thoughts, what she says or her actions rather than just telling the reader.

*Sarah could feel her heart thumping. She walked carefully along the hallway to the kitchen door and listened. Just the hum of the fridge. And the click of the clock. She listened again. But what if the dog was in the kitchen, keeping quiet to fool her? What if it was just waiting for her to creep past the door, to spring out again? She listened harder. Could she hear its breathing? No, that was just the wind outside.*

Really stretch this out. Stress how important it is to build up the readers' suspense by slowing the story down. Another trick in this kind of story is to introduce a surprise. Something startling that turns out to be benign.

*All at once a dark shape leapt out of the kitchen door. It bashed against her with a loud wailing noise. Sarah jumped and screamed as the shape disappeared down the hall. Sarah tried to catch her breath. Then – relief, as she realised what it was. Pringles the cat. She smiled to herself. Fancy being frightened by Pringles. But as Sarah was about to go past the kitchen, another thought came to her. What could possibly have upset the cat so much that it ran out of the kitchen so fast? There was only one thing it could be.*

Explain that in a story the central character should be sympathetic. A reader needs to be able to identify with the main character. The reader also wants a satisfactory ending to the story. And so, although the writer might enjoy having his character come to an unfortunate end, in this case being bitten maybe, he must consider the reader's feelings. This is not to say that all stories should end happily – but they should end satisfactorily. (You might like to discuss this with your writers. What do they think about this? Can they think of any stories they've read that ended unsatisfactorily?)

In this case Sarah and the dog might make friends. Or Mum might arrive home just in time. Perhaps the writer could think of a good twist. The dog saves Pringles from a rat for example. Perhaps it was the rat that scared the cat.

Think of scary locations where a suspense story might be set. Discuss how suspense is handled in books children have read, or in their favourite films or TV shows.

## More about clichés

*Through the magical door*
*I saw roses as red as pillar boxes*
*I saw forget-me-nots as blue as the Chelsea Football Team*
*Daffodils as yellow as cowards*
*Daisies as white as posh hotel sheets*
*And bunny mouths as pink as new-born piglets*

When children begin to write, the use of well-known phrases, sayings and well-worn similes can be useful. However, as we discussed in the redrafting section at the beginning of the book, serious writers seek to avoid clichés at all cost. So, too, with able writers. We must encourage them to be imaginative with language, to seek new ways of expressing themselves and to find fresh, and even surprising, ways to write. Here are four exercises you might try with your able writers.

- As red as a colour

1. Ask the children to compile a list of things that are red, green, blue, yellow, white and black.
2. Now they should write down five common phrases that use colour-related similes. For example, *His face was as red as a beetroot. She went as white as a sheet.*
3. Finally they must substitute the objects in the first list with those in the second. Look for combinations that work – ie still convey the sense of the phrase.

For example, in the phrase *His face was as red as a beetroot* – they might substitute geranium or red-hot lava. Thus getting – *His face was as red as red-hot lava*, or *His face was as red as a geranium*. As red as a geranium would work to describe embarrassment. His face was as red as red-hot lava would certainly describe someone getting very angry.

- The magic garden

Ask the children to imagine they are passing through a secret door into a strange and magical garden. They must describe the things they see using common similes but substituting unusual but fitting words as in the exercise above. The poem could have six, non-rhyming lines, but a regular rhythm. (See the example on page 127.)

Discuss the idea of walking through a magic door. This is itself a cliché of course. Can they think of a better and more unusual way to frame the poem? Challenge them to think of other settings which might be conducive to the creation of a surreal or strange poem. Captured by aliens? Down a manhole? On a moonlit night on holiday on the moor?

● All cut up about clichés

For this you will need a good list of clichés.

Search for clichés on the internet and you'll find several thousand to choose from.

- Distribute blank card or slips of paper – say ten per person.
- Divide into two piles. On each piece of paper in pile A the children must write the object of a cliché. On each piece of paper in pile B they should write its adjective – or its other half.
- Thus pile A might read – BRASS, LAMB, CARPET, GOLD, TREE and pile B – BOLD, HAPPY, RED, GOOD, TALL
- Now collect together all the papers, mix up all the As together and the Bs together and redistribute them.

The object of the exercise is for the children to write a short, one-hundred-word story using those ten words combined in a way that a) is interesting or surprising but that also b) makes sense. (NB This should be fun – remember we're not trying to create a great piece of literature here.)

● Lucy in the Sky with Diamonds

Play *Lucy in the Sky with Diamonds* by the Beatles. Discuss the lyrics. John Lennon was inspired to write this when he saw a picture by his young son who said it was his friend Lucy in the Sky with Diamonds. Write some similar strange and surreal song lyrics to the tune of a popular song. (See *My Not Favourite Things* on page 97.)

# Presenting, performing and publishing

When we visit schools with the 'Able Writers Scheme', we often give a performance at the end of the day for the rest of the school. The four or five groups from other schools, together with the children from the host school, stand at the front and read the poems or extracts from stories that they've written in the day. As well as giving the children encouragement and a boost of confidence it also gives some meaning to their writing. Most writers do what they do because they want to be read and so the reader, and in this case the listener, becomes an important element in any piece of writing.

As well as performing, another way to present children's work is by publishing it in a book. Putting together a book also gives the children a chance to edit their work and to look at it from a fresh perspective. In the same way that the poems and stories are written by able writers you might involve the class artist to illustrate the book, or children who are good at designing to design the book. They could sell the book for a school charity or Children in Need.

After a session working with able writers you might even try brainstorming to come up with other places where their work could be presented, read or listened to. On the internet for example.

# Endword

## An 'Able Writers' group in your school?

As writers who visit schools, we meet many gifted children and always wish that we could work with them for longer than the usual hour-long class workshop. Thus the idea of getting these children together in 'Able Writers' groups seemed an attractive one. It would involve the most able writers from a number of schools joining together in one place to see just how far professional writers could stretch them.

So in early 2002 I talked with Paul Chandler, Head Teacher of St. James' Junior School in Tunbridge Wells, Kent. He told me that his school was a Beacon School and that he had been given a large sum of money to develop projects that would benefit both his school and surrounding schools. I then explained about my plan for Able Writers' days that would happen once a term. Paul was happy to launch the scheme in his school but felt that instead of three times a year, there should be six meetings.

I then contacted other Beacon schools and outlined my idea. Very quickly there were sixteen schemes in operation around the south-east. Tutors were all professional writers – Roy Apps, Clare Bevan, Valerie Bloom, James Carter, Pie Corbett, John Foster, Mike Jubb, Wes Magee, David Orme, Rob Parkinson, John Rice and, of course, Roger Stevens and myself – who were asked to challenge these children, firstly with warm-up activities and then with a longer piece of prose, poetry or script-writing where they could reflect, redraft, discuss and complete something of real worth by the end of the day.

After a couple of years when the Beacon money had been withdrawn, we devised a scheme whereby a host school would have free places but visiting schools would pay per child to attend the sessions, the money raised paying for the writer's fee and expenses.

By 2006 there were almost 50 schemes in operation stretching from Kent to Gloucestershire and north to Nottinghamshire. A Year 2 Able Writers Scheme was also being piloted with five Croydon schools.

# How children benefit

Head Teachers and teachers often comment on how focussed the groups are. This is simply because these are the children who really want to work but are often held back or distracted in normal classroom situations. Everybody stays on task in Able Writers groups because there are no distractions.

Such groups of children inspire and challenge each other as ideas are read aloud and shared from the start. No one is allowed to sit back, there are no passengers in groups such as these, everybody contributes. Socially, too, children enjoy meeting writers from other schools.

Able writers from one school are often surprised and perhaps a little concerned when they realise that there are other children in the group who are as talented as they are. Such 'competition' can only be healthy for the children who are marked out as successes in their own school and who now find they have to try just that little bit harder.

At the end of the day, children and teachers are encouraged to go back to their schools and 'cascade' what they have done so that ideas are spread far beyond the Able Writers groups.

Occasionally we mention the SATs! One Head Teacher told me that these activities would make a real difference in shifting level fours to level fives! Another school rang to say that they had had their best SATs results ever and that they felt that their Able Writers activities had played a big part in achieving those results. Ofsted, too, have praised the Able Writers Schemes in a number of school reports.

*Brian Moses*

*The Able Writers' Scheme is co-ordinated by Trevor Wilson at Authors Abroad/Caboodle Books.*

*If you are interested in becoming a host school for an able writers' group in your area, please contact Trevor on 01535 656015 or email: trevor@caboodlebooks.co.uk*

# Able writers in your school

To run an Able Writers group in your school you can join in the Able Writers Scheme by contacting Brian Moses via Brilliant Publications.

But you can also set up a group of your own. This might involve other schools and getting together for a day with a group of these gifted children and a couple of gifted teachers, or even inviting a professional writer to your school. It might involve simply setting up a group within your school. This would certainly be feasible in a larger school where a mixed group of juniors could meet once or twice a term to write. Yet another alternative would be to set up a writing club, or a poetry club.

Whatever you do, you owe it to your able writers to do something. As Andrew Motion said, in our opening quote, 'the growth of our imagination is central to the growth of our intelligence.'

Good luck.

*Brian Moses and Roger Stevens*

Our websites:
*Brian Moses*
www.brianmoses.co.uk
www.poetryarchive.org

*Roger Stevens*
The Secret Lives of Poets - http://secretlivesofpoets.blogspot.com/
The Poetry Zone -         http://www.poetryzone.co.uk
Blog (for grown-ups) -    http://rogerstevens.blogspot.com
Shop -                    http://www.rabbitpress.com

Brownjohn, S., (1980), *Does it Have to Rhyme?* Hodder & Stoughton.

Dahl. R., (2001), *Revolting Rhymes*, Picture Puffin.

Hughes, T., and Riddell, C., (1988), *Moon-whales*, Faber and Faber.

McCaughrean, G., (2004), *Not the End of the World*, Oxford University Press.

McGough, R., (2000) *The Way Things Are*, Penguin.

Peakes, M., (1999) *A Book of Nonsense*, London, Peter Owen.

Stevens, W., (1954) *The Collected Poems of Wallace Stevens*, New York, Alfred A Knopf.

Stevens, W., (2006), *Collected Poems*, Faber and Faber.

Tyler, A., (1988), *Breathing Lessons*, Pan Books.

Wiliams, W. C., (1938) *Collected Poems: 1909–1939, Volume* 1, New York, New Directions Publishing Corp.

Williams, W.C., (2000), *Selected Poems*, Penguin Classics.

Yates, C., (1999), *Jumpstart*, The Poetry Society.

# Index of Poetry & Prose

Able Writers in Your School

# School Acknowledgements

Our thanks to the schools whose pupils contributed to this book:

Amherst Junior School, St. Peter Port, Guernsey,
Blewbury Endowed C of E Primary School, Didcot, Oxfordshire,
Cavendish School, Eastbourne, East Sussex,
Claverham Community College, Battle, East Sussex,
Corpus Christi Catholic Primary School, Bournemouth,
Elston Junior School, Gosport, Hampshire,
Etchingham School, Etchingham, East Sussex,
Eton End School, Datchet, Windsor,
Farnsfield St. Michael's Primary School, Farnsfield, Nottinghamshire,
Heron Way Primary School, Horsham, West Sussex,
Holy Trinity C of E Primary School, Ramsgate, Kent,
Horndean Junior School, Horndean, Hampshire,
Hunton Primary School, Hunton, Kent,
Longlevens Junior School, Longlevens, Gloucester,
Muskham Primary School, North Muskham, Nottinghamshire,
Nine Mile Ride Primary School, Wokingham, Berkshire,
Ocklynge Junior School, Eastbourne, East Sussex,
Queen Edith Community Primary School, Cambridge,
Queen Eleanor Junior School, Guildford, Surrey,
Selston Bagthorpe Primary School, Bagthorpe, Nottinghamshire,
South Moreton Primary School, South Moreton, Oxfordshire,
St. Anne's Catholic Primary, Banstead, Surrey,
St. James' CE Junior School, Tunbridge Wells,
St. James the Great Catholic Primary School, Peckham, Greater London,
St. John's CE Primary School, Crowborough, East Sussex,
St. Martin's Primary School, Dover, Kent,
St. Matthew's CE Primary School, Tunbridge Wells, Kent,
St. Peter's CEP School, East Bridgeford, Nottinghamshire,
Sutton High School, Sutton, Surrey,
Tavistock & Summerhill Preparatory School, Haywards Heath, West Sussex,
Winthorpe Primary School, Winthorpe, Nottinghamshire.

Note: All examples are by children in Years 5 and 6 unless otherwise stated.
If anyone else feels that they should have been credited in this book, please contact Brilliant Publications and amendments will be made in subsequent editions.

*Also thanks to Anne Moses for her help in the development of the Able Writers Scheme and to Jill Stevens for her editing skills.*

Lightning Source UK Ltd.
Milton Keynes UK
UKOW02f0801111214

242934UK00002B/35/P